THE EMPATHETIC ATTORNEY

ADVOCATING FOR SURVIVORS OF SEXUAL
VIOLENCE THROUGH TRAUMA INFORMED CARE

ANNAMARIE MOTIS

Cover Design: Jennifer Stimson

Editing: Cory Hott

CONTENTS

For Erin, For Sean.
This – all because of your empathy.

THE HELPERS

There's a quiet conference room on the ground level of a 1910s craftsman home in Portland, Oregon. There sit three attorneys. The focus of their congregation that mid-morning – a young woman, victim to sexual misconduct by the hand of a member of the Board of Trustees where she was attending college; the reason for their congregation, to conduct an interview for a Title IX Investigation. The young woman had already been through multiple interviews with the police department. She had been asked to recreate the scene, to relive the moments of assault in the presence of others; she had already traded her privacy and individuality for the sake of the investigation, and here, she was being asked to do so yet again.

The first attorney was logical. All the right words were employed to give the victim a sense of security. "You are in control here." "We're going at your pace." "I'm here to document your experience." But once questions started being asked, it became apparent that sympathetic understanding was not at the center of the attorney's questions.

Consideration for how questions would impact the victim were disregarded, and phrasing seemed overtly inconsiderate of the fact this was supposed to be an unbiased investigation.

The other two attorneys were empathetic. When the first attorney asked blunt questions, they rephrased them in a way they knew would be more approachable to the victim's experience. When sensing overwhelming emotions, they interjected for a break without the victim having to request themselves. Their understanding of the needs of the investigator were refined by their understanding of the impact of trauma and thus, they could effectively help the victim communicate their needs to the external world.

In order to understand the experience of another, the discomfort present in their life and the stress complicating everyday actions, one must learn to empathize – and empathize intelligently. Empathy is far too often confused with sympathy, and sympathy is far too often considered an emotion of the vulnerable. Sympathy is the ability to relate to another's circumstance, at minimum, feeling reciprocal feelings with another. Sympathy is an important element to empathy, but you can sympathize with another's sadness without understanding such sadness. You can feel another's pain without understanding how they are being impacted by such pain. Empathy is the ability to *understand* another's experience. Empathy is needed to go beyond sharing emotion and clue into the genesis of it all. Think of your existing ability to sympathize as your existing ability to walk; you are born with this talent, you learned by witnessing others. Empathy then, becomes your ability to run. All of us *can* run, some with more or less natural ability than others; but regardless of natural talent, there are those who have developed tremendous abilities to perfect the skill.

Empathy is much like running. Naturally, we find ourselves faced with emotion as a simple element of our humanity; intelligent empathy takes practice. By communicating ourselves to a deeper understanding of the impact of trauma, we develop our skill to best serve the victims for which our skill is dedicated.

THE RECKONING

"Would suing him impeded my ability to campaign for public office someday?" If you have been sitting in a consultation and your client has asked you a question like this, I can only imagine the list of responses that run through your head. How could I possibly predict what impact this incident will have on this person's life? Is future reputation regarding an impact on a campaign really their main concern right now? Potentially running for a public office one day? Don't they care more about finding retribution? Justice?

I can only imagine the flood of responses Sean had during our consultation. I had always been the person in a place of advocacy for others; until I found myself incapable of helping even myself. Searching for understanding and accountability in the wake of monumental injustice, I found a gladiator to enter the battle on my behalf; someone to fight not only for the pursuit of justice, but for wholistic restitution. Sitting in his office that first day, I felt as if I was face to face with the suited soldier version of Bruce Willis. I'm not sure meeting the actual man himself would have been any less daunting; for I was outside of my body with anticipation, concern, worry, dread, and embarrassment. His empathetic approach ensured that I knew there was someone to guide me through my confusion and anger, to navigate the daunting system ahead, to bring the reckoning long overdue.

This was the first time somebody was listening to my exact needs and taking them on as if they were their own. My anticipation, concern, worry, dread, and embarrassment still existent – but I was not alone in carrying the burden or navigating the halls of justice I sought.

I didn't not realize at the time I hadn't but one gladiator in the arena. I stood amidst a congregation of gladiators, armed in their battle for those unable to fight for themselves. Each with their own unique expertise, fending the foes that threaten a victim's ability to heal post mortal injury. Finding oneself a victim of sexual assault is to receive a life sentence; a sentence that takes time to understand why it was placed on you as victim instead of them as perpetrator. While each approach to advocacy is formed from unique perspective, every advocate struggles with the same question daily – how do I address the victims' legal needs in the most effective way possible while minimizing continued trauma?

Those on the outside, interacting with those victimized by a broad scale of trauma inflicted on an individual due to sexual violence, have the luxury of viewing the victims experience from a holistic perspective. The helpers of the trauma world, have a great ability to influence the extent of healing that takes place in a victim's life after such a traumatic event. Helpers can see how short sighted, or potentially how farsighted, a victim's questions may be in the midst of navigating their current landscape. Humans have great ability to adapt. Trauma does not always equal negative lifelong effects, but one's ability to heal from the date of damage does depend on the circumstance in which the victim finds themselves victimized, and finds themselves responded to amid the traumatic circumstance. This is why the existence of empathetic helpers is so vital to ensuring that survivors of sexual trauma are just that – survivors – instead of victimized individuals coping with the impacts of trauma.

HONEY BADGER DOES CARE

It was the summer of 2020. As the world was experiencing great pause due to the pandemic in place, I found myself opening a small tasting room outside of Carlton, Oregon for a husband and wife operated winery. As I welcomed a small group inside of the tasting room attached to the winery operation, we dove into common pleasantries about where the guests were from, how they heard about Chris James Cellars and sequentially what they did for a living. The man's name was James, and as soon as he commented that he was a DA, my mind drifted, collecting potential questions. Mentioning a relationship with a few counties that were familiar to me, even given my short time in Oregon, something struck me to impose the question, had he ever worked with an Erin Greenawald? A verbal response was not necessary as his face showed instant signs of recognition, mingled with shock as eventually a verbal response did come: "You mean the honey badger?"

Never had I heard such a uniquely accurate complement. Honey badger indeed – Erin embodies the creature's reputation for relentless pursuit against virtually any enemy. Going back to the room with the three attorneys – it was as if Erin was fighting in a war and dancing in a ballet at the same time. With seamless effort, she interpreted the statements of the first attorney in a manner that first, made clear the shortcomings of the original statement while second, offered me the ability to formulate a response based on a question I could sincerely understand. This may have been the first, but it was not nearly the last time I witnessed her ability to empathetically proctor conversations. Time and time again, she gracefully validated my position as victim while offering greater understanding of the process; not only providing me with the necessary advocacy to learn to heal, but simultaneously offering those in witness an example of how empathetic advocacy is achievable if practiced intentionally.

> *Hi AnnaMarie,*
>
> *I wanted to just check in with you and see how you're doing? If you want to talk before tomorrow's interview, we can do that this evening, or we can meet tomorrow morning around 8:20 or so before Ms. Starr arrives. Just let me know.*
>
> *I can appreciate that anticipating the interview would be really stressful. From my point of view, just know that I have complete confidence in you and your ability to communicate honestly and clearly about what was done to you; this interview is simply another opportunity for you to tell your truth.*
>
> *I hope you're able to enjoy the day at least a little bit. I see the sunshine is starting to peek out.*
>
> *Talk to you soon,*
>
> *Erin*

This email from Erin is one of my favorite examples of how her words always seemed to offer validation with combined assurance that the world was not ending. She recognized my need for motherly compassion, but never let the boundaries blur as in her position of attorney.

VICTIM TO SURVIVOR

I was incredibly fortunate to have been led to advocates who embody trauma informed care before I even understood what that term implied. They embodied the practice, they *are* the industry leaders and national examples of trauma informed advocacy. With every phone call, email, interview, in every element of their approach toward me as client, I never doubted their care regarding my legal needs was centered on their desire for me to find healing. They intentionally considered the impact of every interaction within the legal sphere and how such interaction would impact my efforts to move past my victimization and enter the life of a survivor.

When you find yourself walking alongside the victim of sexual assault, be it in your professional role or personal journey, a need is generated to become fluent in two contradicting languages – victim mentality and legal lingo When a victim of sexual assault finds themself seeking adversary from the legal system, they often approach the search for justice as if their healing was dependent upon timely resolution. What is difficult to understand when you're in a place of victimization is that one's search for healing cannot be reliant upon a system that offers no guarantee of justice, for justice is defined by all involved differently. The legal system guarantees procedural review of a specific occurrence, but it doesn't guarantee the eye-for-an-eye approach most victims would desire. The search for healing must be conducted simultaneously with the search for justice, but independently to be sustainable outside of the ultimate resolution. Those within the legal system or in its supporting institutions, often assume that the individual vocalizing they're abuse has already transformed from victim to survivor. The mindset of a victim must be understood and respected on its own separate from the mindset of a survivor. Unbraiding the relationship between criminal justice and personal justice is critical to ensure the victim is equipped with the best tools for healing. It is my hope that through the following pages you'll be able to gain insight into the victim mindset in order to conduct your practice in a more effective way to help victim find their survivor status.

2

THE POWER OF A SMALL COLLEGE

THIS ISN'T THE AIRPORT

"Please place your bag on the conveyor belt and take any metal you have, placing it in the bin." As you waited your turn in line to place your belongings into a plastic container your mind floods with thoughts such as, *Are there any random piece of metal that I forgot did I get the keys.* As you watch your belongings enter the black box, your mind races with a little panic even though you know that there is no reason for concerned. You approach the body scanner, asking quickly, "Is my belt going to make it go off? Is this okay?" You grabbed a few belongings. You had taken off shoes, belts, and your bag and stepped to the side to assemble yourself once again and proceed down the halls toward your destination.

I believe it's safe to assume that most people saw themselves into the airport terminal described in the above scenario. I mean, where else does one interact with metal scanners to ensure the safety of the public? I have a great number of similar memories on my way to incredible destinations. That's not what I think of anymore. Every time that I have to navigate security a piece of me that still worries about seeing him unexpectedly.

The last time I went through security and remember the day vividly was the day that I entered the courthouse to attend my abuser's sentencing. I walked through the security of the courthouse, grabbed my bag off of the conveyor belt, adjusting my shoes only to turn around and see him. He was sitting right there, adjusting his shoes. He had just finished as he looked up to realize I was standing there. We both froze. I still hear the security guard talking to the other people in line, small talk, the low hum of the conveyor belt, shoes echoing down distant halls.

I still feel frozen.

The rewiring of my brain to trigger fear in a situation fear is unnecessary provides evidence of the biological impact of trauma. When a human endures an experience outside of their consent that is so extreme or repetitive, they will learn to adapt to the trauma in attempt to minimize experienced pain. Internalizing trauma impacts a victim's association with the external world, causing that which was once harmless to become painful stimuli, causing not only emotional but legitimate physical distress. Understanding the needs of victim's requires the ability to not simply feel compassion for those struggling in the wake of abuse, but to embrace their status as victim, validate their experience and offer practical guidance on their transformative journey to find their survivor identity.

SINFIELD

The morning wind snagged a strand of hair, whipping it across rosy, numb cheeks. Growing up on the edge of the

Arctic Circle, I anticipated heat and selected a tank-top that morning. No coat. Be it mid-August in the Willamette Valley, the night air still lingered in the shadows cast by Melrose Hall. It is on these steps I sat at 5:30 am August 21, 2016 – alone, if not for my two suitcases, duffel, and backpack, oh, and the book in hand. Every incoming class at Linfield College was required to read a common title, ours, *The Circle*. As an eighteen-year-old inherently pessimistic about the rise of social media, I was eager to devour Dave Eggers' every word through the fictional parable. Orientation was not supposed to begin till 8:30. The doors were locked, but I fret not as that gave me a whole two-and-a-half hours to find and mark my favorite passages for discussion. If my cheeks hadn't been struck by the effect of the wind, I might not have even remembered it was present.

At some point just after 7:00, I startled a slender gentleman with a kind face as he approached Melrose's steps, head down. Fumbling through keys, he looked up and exclaimed, "I'm sorry I didn't see you! Good morning! I take it you're an early arrival for orientation this morning. How long have you been here?" As he helped roll my luggage into the Fred Meyer Lounge, I explained how I was from Alaska and had flown in from Anchorage that morning. After tucking me into a corner, he explained how the rest of the morning would look and some of the different people I would be meeting. Before he left, I asked his name as I thanked him profusely for such a warm welcome. Smiling humbly, he replied, "My name is Dan."

I had the privilege of working with Dan through my countless positions held while at Linfield. First as the founder and president of the yoga club, I found an itch to become more involved with student life. After serving in over twelve unique positions/departments for Linfield, I would feel confident claiming Linfield administration as my family away from home. It wasn't until I found myself victim and witness in a sexual assault scandal, leading to a daunting wave of truth, that Dan's seemingly sudden retirement a short time prior made sense. He was the first to receive an official report of the sexual misconduct of a member of the Board of Trustees.

I was that board member's next victim.

Before Jubb's sandpaper hands had time to transform the relationship that I had with Linfield from constructive to destructive, there had been nearly three years of layered relationships built with the individuals and the administration staff faculty and student communities. I had been at Linfield minor weeks before I began the process for creating the Yoga Club. Through the club creation process, I identified areas of frustration and thought to myself, *Why not be a part of the solution instead of complaining?*

This led to becoming the club director for the student government. What was unique about Linfield student government, known as ASLC, was that we operated licensed as a 501(c)3 nonprofit organization. It was the unique structure of this organization that placed me into the position to act as liaison between administrative needs and student desires. According to both ASLC and Linfield bylaws, the vice president of ASLC served as a member of the Linfield Board of Trustees, with all voting rights and privileges. By the time I found myself elected to this position, I had found myself involved in nearly every corner of the campus.

I understood the experience of niche clubs on campus because I had founded the yoga club.

I understood the vast spectrum of student interests and needs because I was club director.

I understood student event planning as I was the chair of the activities council.

I understood the athletes of our community because I joined alongside the women's basketball team as a manager.

I understood the unique sport culture within administration because I ran official bookkeeping at men and women's basketball games.

I understood the underappreciated and thankless positions behind the scenes within administration because I worked for the Department of Human Resources.

I understood the wide array of support and guidance needed for even the most successful student when it came to thinking beyond academia because I worked over the summer months for the Office of Career Development.

I understood the importance of generating pride in my alma mater when I traveled through summer months as a student ambassador.

I understood the importance of bonding with like-minded women, striving to set an example of excellence in personal and professional pursuits as a member of the Alpha Phi Fraternity.

I understood the impact of integrating into the greater community we found ourselves within through seeking avenues for service to the residents of McMinnville and beyond.

It was this very understanding of the community which I served that I assumed would carry weight when I made the first report of misconduct. It was these very people who had given me their friendship and confidence that turned to insinuate I was responsible for creating such a catastrophic circumstance.

FLAT TIRE

I was driving back from Portland, just finishing an internship interview. It wasn't raining at the time, but I know that it had rained earlier that day. I remember that distinct sound of tires on a wet road. Being maybe twenty minutes away from campus running through my mind of what needed to happen next. I was interrupted by a phone call. It was a good friend, Nat, who explained she had a flat tire and didn't feel confident addressing the situation on her own. I assured her that I would be there in less than twenty minutes, I arrived, stepped out of my Volvo to find her face in complete shock. I approached her in my floral lined, black, Ann Taylor pantsuit with three-and-a-half-inch black pumps, prepared to remedy a flat.

I changed countless flats around campus, hypothetically and literally. Looking back, I believe I was more preoccupied with facilitating an incredible student experience for everyone else than I was with enjoying my own experience. Outside of class time, I would have anywhere from four to fourteen meetings a week. I formed a close relationship with the college president, taking pride in his position of mentorship. We bonded over shared trauma and outlier status. Members of the Board of Trustees offered advanced promises for letters of recommendation for my post-graduate law school pursuits. I formed relationships with individuals from every corner of campus, every sub-culture and community. Perhaps one relationship too many.

THE INCIDENT

"Hey, Anna Marie! This is the trustee I wanted to introduce you to. This is David Jubb." February 15th plays through my mind like one's most current music obsession. I remember the moments before meeting Jubb the most. It was the February congregation for the board as there were three every year. After a long Friday of sessions and committee reports, there was a cocktail hour held in a lobby which coincidentally enough was my academic department political science. This cocktail hour was supposed to be a social between board members and faculty staff as there had been tensionless relations due to the transition of the new president and rumors of university status and merging. I was talking with a professor who I was quite fond of when he asked about my plans post-graduation. After explaining my interest in pursuing the international transactional side of the corporate world it dawned on him to introduce me to a board member who he thought would be a great resource in that pursuit. Jubb's initial conversation with me seemed to be focus on the qualities of leadership I am bodied and the great resource he could be because of his experience and relationship with influential individuals.

"Do you want another glass? Why even ask? We need another bottle. Hold on, let me get the cash." Across the dinner table, I watched Jubb shuffle through hundred-dollar bills stuffed into a white envelope, fondling what he thought appropriate to hand the waitress. After cocktail hour, everyone had carpooled to the Michelbook Golf Course where dinner was served to the congregation of faculty and trustees. The glasses sitting on the end of the table in proximity to Jubb were never empty, regardless of who's setting to which they belonged. In the moment, I attributed his generosity to his personality – everyone I had ever met in association with Linfield was someone anyone would call good people. Linfield was a community built on excellence, fostering excellence through education, attracting only excellent people. Once a member of a community, one naturally lets initial guards down, as community is a social contract of shared interest and well-being. Only after the incident was I told, "Jubb is a good guy, as long as he's not drunk."

Post-Friday dinner, the good-ole-boys club met in a backroom of a restaurant in downtown McMinnville. While I have no prior history of agenda subjects, I assumed content for the large board meeting the following morning was regularly a subject of conversation. Given I was sharing a rather exciting proposal the following day, when asked to join the inner circles' intimate gathering, I readily accepted. I was armed with information and determined to gain the support of the key few to support my approach to the many. As the end of dinner approached, arrangements were made surrounding the carpool onto the restaurant. While I thought plans had been solidified, I quickly excused myself to the bathroom; only to return and find the group had left, save Jubb. He explained he didn't want to get in the car with someone that had even a drop of alcohol and thought it best we Uber on our own. Here again, I assumed his genuine intention was to be protective of me as a current student; when he made the request for me to call an Uber, he was doing so to keep me from a precarious situation. He handed me two twenty-dollar bills. When I initially said that's okay, this is too much, he told me it can be a tip.

Those that know McMinnville know that scheduling an Uber is just about as convenient as going down to the DMV and registering a completely new car bought for the specific purpose of getting you from point A to point B. Those of you who know me will know my experience with the technical world is less than babies born tomorrow, so when Uber approximated the arrival time of my driver to three minutes, I relayed the information and proposed we wait outside. When those three minutes near tripled in time, I suggested we wait in the lobby as I noticed him leaning closer toward me. Another assumption – I assumed his instability was due to a combination of his stature and intoxication level and offered support. When I felt his hand run down between my asscheeks, I pushed away with confusion. "That's definitely not something I'm comfortable with." in response to his initial assault. Be it a conditioned symptom of victimization or femininity, but my initial reaction was to assume I was misreading the situation. My initial response was calculated as to make him aware I was not interested in further pursuit without diminishing his masculinity or place of authority – both instinctively deserving my reverence.

His response was to return inside "for more wine." As I stood waiting in the lobby, I was trying to mentally process what had happened as a faculty member who sat next to me at dinner opened the door. "Is everything okay? Are you okay? I just noticed you hadn't left and was wondering if you needed a ride." This faculty member, along with her friend, must have sensed manipulation in the air – but I assured them we simply needed a ride downtown to join the others. I had made myself clear to him; why would he try again? I wasn't going to let his behavior prevent me from gaining the ear of the others. When Jubb returned from his chardonnay scavenge, he was carrying two Styrofoam cups full of all the oaky buttery-ness one can tell simply from the nose (have you ever smelt warm chard in Styrofoam?). I placed the cup I was given in the corner of my purse as we arranged ourselves in her car, me sitting in back with the friend, Jubb riding in the front as passenger. Once at the rendezvous location downtown, we learned that the restaurant was currently closed after an unfortunate flooding. An alternative location was suggested, one with a much less intimate atmosphere. We convened at the busy bar; the kind with thin, long high-top tables that provided college students and the younger professionals a space to decompress after the week's responsibility. Five of us ultimately sat together at one end of those tables, me directly across from Jubb. The table was so thin that the seat edges nearly touched when pushed under the table, so when containing a human body with legs and knees, there was a necessity to push your chair back when seated to create space. I pushed out my chair and turned it slightly, as to create more space away from who's knees mine were colliding. Focused on the conversation, I felt my chair being adjusted but not by myself. One second, I was confused by the movement, the next I was penetrated by sandpaper fingers as he jabbed his hand into my crotch. Instantaneously, I pushed away from the table and with the same breath, informed everyone that I suddenly didn't feel well and needed to leave. The moments between the foreign fingers against my delicate lips and me finding a way home felt as though I was navigating an escape from a sudden explosion. The ring in your ears when your mind is incapable of processing what information it's just received; aware danger surrounds and thus a single pursuit of finding safety.

When your body is penetrated without given consent, you experience the ultimate form of violation. Being the victim of physical assault is never questioned – no one would wish ill will on themselves, right? Seeing is believing; seeing someone's physical pain triggers basic instinctual empathy. Proclaiming you are a victim of sexual assault is met with much more resistance. Doubt rises in the minds of others because they subconsciously question that person's sexual desires.

Consent is the difference between sexual assault and sexual interest.

Without consent, even the most objectively romantic action violates individuality.

Saturday came. My one thought was to get through the day. Just to get through the presentation. I could process when I could clear my mind and focus on me, but in that moment, I had a student body who's interests needed an advocate. I managed to avoid any direct contact with Jubb until the mid-morning break. He caught me in the Starbucks line, paying for my coffee and that of another in line. It was his comment on the walk back to the board room that will play through my mind over any other words from that weekend – "last night was fun, wasn't it?"

The following Monday I identified my course of action. Even being involved in the Linfield community as I was, I was frankly not sure of who to talk to or who to bring a report. Eventually I found myself reporting to a woman viewed as a mother-figure among Linfield's administrative body, who also happened to be the Title IX coordinator. After recounting the incident, I indicated that I would be reporting to the police and thought she should start the necessary procedure within the institution. A meeting was immediately set up between me and the chair of the board of trustees to address what had happened. In our private conversation he told me that he had long been concerned for his friend's state of alcoholism. He validated my abuse through the fact that he was not shocked by the things that his friend even allegedly did while intoxicated, *and* that he had noticed there was movement at that end of the table, he just thought I was fidgety. He convinced me that this incident was damning enough to his friend's reputation that he would be immediately removed from the board and that no other individual let alone student would be put into a position should be harmed by this man again.

If only I knew when I walked through those doors after the meeting that I would become the target for Linfield's anger and fear of the past surfacing, I would have conducted myself and such a different manner. But. I gave the institution that I had committed my life to the benefit of the doubt; it would give me its best advocacy as I had always given it the best of myself.

INSTITUTIONAL BETRAYAL

The concept of institutional betrayal refers to the wrongful actions perpetrated toward an individual by an institution that they had historically felt obligations to and from. This concept is best understood when comparing it to that of our immune system. Harmonious operation between bodily systems functions indefinitely. The instant something within our system is found to be out of balance, threat is imposed. Even being the threat is our body itself, our immune system will relentlessly target what it believes is the cause of the threat until the threat is eliminated.

Linfield betrayed me on a multitude of levels – but it wasn't the community itself. That I believe still exists, despite what efforts of the administration are made to mold its existence into the best functioning business possible. It was individual actors who each made the choice to protect their positions, their departments. Linfield's immune system targeted me as though I was responsible for their own oversights in holding members of the community accountable to its own value statements.

Jennifer Freed is a psychologist at the University of Oregon and is the founder and president for the Center of Institutional Courage. Her book, *Blind to Betrayal,* illustrates the impact that institutional action has on the psychology of an individual. The concept of DARVO outlines how, when threat to an institution is identified that institution, it will deny any existence of the threat and will attack those responsible for identifying the threat by reversing victim and offender positions. This restructure of actors serves to detour accountability and generate misplaced empathy. DARVO can occur on the smallest of scales, be it simply by a boss that demands loyalty but undermines individuality, or to the extent of Linfield where major attacks are made towards the individuals deemed threatening.

My truth of falling victim to the hand of a longstanding member of Linfield's Board was an incredible threat to the institution itself. It quickly became apparent that my report of Jubb's misconduct was not being investigated or being considered with much weight. The initial promises I had received from Baca had merely been an attempt to patch a hole in a dyke that had no business being patched at all. This was structural damage being treated as cosmetic – and there was no way I could be the only one to see that fact. I gained more insight from long standing Linfield community members. I learned of incidents on campus involving his inappropriate conduct with both female and male students.

I knew I had not been the first and I knew if I didn't do something I wouldn't be the last.

I knew if I did not do something it would not be the last time I felt victim to another's hand.

Administrative members later validated my experience to a new degree when evidence was presented, confirming previous reports of sexual misconduct had been filed against Jubb. The response for knowing full-well Jubb was a perpetrator and knowing full-well my position as student trustee posed threat was to have us sit close enough together to keep an eye on us both at the same time.

BEING SEA BLONDE

When I tell people I grew up on the edge of the Arctic Circle, most look at me and my velvet dress as if I just tried to convince them that the sky isn't blue. My mind turns to my dad's favorite story of how I ever so gently hit a young muskox that popped up from a ravine while he was first teaching me to drive a truck. The conversation always leads into one being asked what a Musk ox even is and to in turn describing said creature as a massive shaggy horned hamster. Being as this gives no real illustration or mental picture to the majority of humans on the planet, the conversation usually ends up somewhere along the lines of how strange or how peculiar or what an anomaly Anna-Marie is, and it's her essence. I suppose a lot of that uniqueness is owed to the place that I formed my world-view. But every time I hear someone comment about how I interact with the world in a strange and unique way, what I hear is that I'm failing to behave normal and I'm the only one who knows why I'll never be normal.

Given my unique homeland, one should not be surprised to find out my experience at Linfield was not my first experience of assault. it was merely the first time I was in a position to advocate for myself. I was born on Kodiak Island, known as the Emerald Isle, situated off the southern coast of Alaska. Here I spent my first ten years amidst the grizzly bear and the mountain goats. Weeks before my tenth birthday, we moved to the mainland where I lived outside of Soldotna and Kenai for about another year before moving to Homer. By my thirteenth birthday, I found myself blowing out those candles in a new home – an apartment on top of the grocery store my father managed in Nome. It was in this two-bedroom-stretched -to three where I lived with five other siblings (the sixth being older and already moved-away). During the first month or so that I spent a Nome, I remember my mom sending me out of the house with specific instructions not to return until I had a job a paying job. Unable to determine if my tears were from the cold for simple realization of growing up, I found motivation to become more financially independent and worked for a micro spa in town ran by a beautiful woman named Trinh. She became my role model, as I worked alongside her in the spa and eventually in her newly established floral shop (serving the greater Norton Sound area). This position as an unofficial personal assistant over my six years in Nome was key in my professional development; but what was only apparent to me after my experience with Linfield – I was developing a shell of coping mechanisms.

I never had the choice of losing my virginity. Coming from a devout Christian family – I never considered that there was anyone to blame for what happened, save for myself. My shame and guilt manifested itself into my pursuit of control for the world around me. My experience developed a sense of risk aversion which landed itself incredibly useful in both academic and professional pursuits. I couldn't study for a trigonometry test without considering every possible route for my failure; I couldn't help identify a bride selection for her wedding flowers without considering every possible way in which a decision could be made wrong. When I found myself victim at the hand of not only Linfield's board member but at Linfield's actions itself, I already knew that I knew how to navigate feeling victimized. The only difference was that I knew how to develop the mentality of a survivor instead of learning to cope as victim.

3

INTELLIGENTLY CONCEIVED
WARFARE

As you find yourself walking alongside victims of sexual assault – if they read not but a single book in preparation for their fight for justice, it should be *The Art of War*. An ancient Chinese manuscript outlining militaristic strategy, these thirteen chapters give the reader practical advice in engaging with an adversary and bullet form. While one may expect the focus of such a manuscript to be difficult to translate into modern day legal warfare, the essence of this book is to find and respect the beauty that lies in artfully navigating conflict with respect for both friend and foe in their positions of actors within the reality we exist. To engage in battle is to engage in the defense of what one believes is true and just and righteous. When we find ourselves engaged in battle with such a purpose, it is foolish to assume that the opposing party is doing so with the lack of the same motivation. Because the driving force of each party is rooted in elements of morality, is easy for one to feel they are being undermined and criticized instead of the nature of the reality of the trauma caused. *The Art of War* can help a victim understand to separate their need for or emotional healing from pursuits within the criminal justice system and see their efforts within the legal system as synonymous with that of conducting ancient warfare. One of my favorite reminders is found in the reminder to know oneself, to know the enemy. Knowing these two actors can only be realized by paying attention. When I know I need to focus my attention, I try and take a moment to separate myself from the swarming environment I'm seated.

What are five things you can see?

Give yourself permission to just look at your surroundings. Don't think about the next to-do, that carries you out of the present. Tell your attention we will be here for a while, staying present.

What are four things you can touch?

Allowing ourselves to tune into the physical ways we are in contact with our surroundings allows our attention to focus on what is immediate. Focus your attention to what is grounding you here and now.

What are three things you can hear?

Sound penetrates our subconscious more than we will ever recognize. We live in a time where silence truly is golden, as our environments are polluted with the constant hum of countless decibels. Finding the skill to focus on specific noise will help your mind stay present.

What are two things you can smell?

We often forget about our nose till it's needed, sensing intense aroma when present. Learning to identify less potent, more subtle scents will strengthen your ability to keep your mind centered on the here and now.

What is one thing you can taste?

This one can seem a little silly. Obviously, if I'm not

eating or drinking, what could I be tasting? I'll tell you this – flavor can be detected on the tongue simply by way of memory. Coach yourself to untangle the flood of sensory information it's receiving to hone-in your palate. Can you detect the cold coffee consumed hours after being heated up thrice in a row, only to be forgotten? Can you taste that favorite dinner you requested tonight for dinner?

Learning to focus on the present will enable you to manage the difficult conversations about to be had surrounding the reality of living as a victim of sexual assault. In the wake of significant trauma, we find ourselves needing to adapt to a new normal level of discomfort – stress.

Healthy stress. Yes, this is such a thing. In a world where success is ever defined by what can be externally validated, we find ourselves encountering genuine stress on a daily basis. Stress derived from expectation. Expectation to do our best, to present, preform, promote the best of ourselves in every window of our worlds. We all understand stress. But perhaps.

Not everyone understands the degree of stress one finds themselves under when navigating the stress of processing their trauma; compounded by the requirement of engaging with the inherently stressful system of American justice. This stress is not felt simply because it's uncomfortable. The stress of PTSD roots itself in a victim's biology, reshaping the way they view and interact with their world. Without an understanding the nature of trauma, victims will encounter those advocates with genuine hearts of concern, acting without a wholistic perspective into what a victim truly needs, from who, when. By embracing the impact of trauma, advocates can approach victims in a method best conducive for their healing. The first step of this process, setting expectations for what is to come.

WHAT DID I SIGN-UP FOR EXACTLY?

Early in my college experience, and I should say very early for it was probably only the first six weeks of my freshman year that I had any free time, but a handful of times, I found myself randomly walking into the movie theater. I would look up at the current releases and simply pick a title piquing my interest. While Nome had a movie theater (it was also the subway), it was usually the only one playing for a few weeks. Being in Oregon and having a theater with five screens? That was just beyond my comprehension. This one day in particular, I found myself itching for an experience with Avenger-like-individuals and quickly selected the title I thought would lead me toward the action. Twenty minutes passed before it becomes apparent to me that I was not sitting in a film gearing up for great superhero conflict resolution, but instead was watching an emotional reenactment about the Boston Marathon bombing. While my first thought was that I had walked into the wrong theatre, turns out, everything was on the up and up. I just didn't have the right expectation.

FROM THE GET-GO

My expectation for this book is that you are able to understand the victim experience to a deeper level so that you can be more effective in your communication with survivors. We will walk through basic legal terminology, not for the purpose of increasing our vocabulary but for the purpose of understanding what each of those terms means to a victim and their specific relationship to the victims' experience. We will navigate the first ninety days of a lawsuit, we will navigate official investigations, long-lasting legal pursuit, and the aftermath once resolution is found. All these events approached from the victim's perspective, what unique challenges they face and how to best offer support.

Setting expectations – be it before a meeting to simply outline what the meeting will include, or be it to have a meeting wholly focused on setting expectations for the legal process – may be the most critical element to establishing the best grounds possible for victim healing. When navigating the emotional title wave assault causes one to endure, it can be challenging separating the punishment you want in your view of justice from the reality of possible outcomes. When interacting with victims, it is crucial you share expectations for possible outcomes without making definite statements, and by offering a wide scope of possibilities. It can seem as though reassuring the victim justice will be served will reinforce assurance in their place as victim. However, suggesting broad ideas of justice and accountability often set the victim up for disappointment down the road, when their view of such is contrary to probable outcomes.

Sexual assault victims exist in a world of doubt. Doubt demonstrates itself in a victim's inability to vocalize their needs or their truth and can even extend to doubt that they are deserving of advocacy or justice for their situation in the first place. Regardless of the position you hold in the victim's pursuit for justice, it is vital that they be confident of and not doubt what your role in their life is, no doubt what the objective of a meeting is or engage with misconception. Reassure them, constantly, they are not a burden. They will never be able to hear those words enough. "*You are not a burden.*"

The importance of expectations was demonstrated to me through my attorneys from the first moment we met. Sean and Erin used their understanding of trauma to approach every interaction with me, even that of their emails. One of the most valuable, tangible examples of them prioritizing clear expectations was their practice of emailing summaries after phone calls. I'll always prefer to speak over the phone, but in the midst of mental cloudiness, found it challenging to retain every piece of information. Post phone call, I always received an e-mail stating what had been said, what their next course of action would be and what was currently expected of me. This practice started not three minutes after I had signed and submitted my contingent fee agreement with Sean.

March 12, 2019
12:31 p.m.

Good afternoon,

I'd like to schedule a meeting to ask a few more questions before committing to a course of action. I'm available Thursday morning before 12:30, or Friday before 1:00. If neither of those times work for you, let me know and I'll make something work. Thank you so very much!

Ever forward,
AnnaMarie

12:41 p.m.

Ms. Motis

Good to hear from you. I am out of town starting tomorrow at noon. I am available the rest of the afternoon and by phone Thursday and Friday.

Sean Riddell

3:46 p.m.

Hello again,

   You'll find my signed Contingent Fee Agreement attached to this email.

   Ever forward,
   AnnaMarie

3:49pm

The detective assigned to your matter is going to email me tomorrow, as will the victim's advocate from the DA's office. They agreed to conduct your interview at my office. We will discuss dates and times later this week. I will be in military orders starting tomorrow, but accessible via my phone all weekend.

   Sean

My gladiator was advocating for my needs as soon as I vocalized acceptance for such advocacy. Not only was my gladiator advocating for my needs through setting clear expectations on my behalf, but also through his advocacy of needs that I did not even recognize at the time. In these first e-mails from my attorney, he was advocating for the victim mindset knowing I would be impacted by entering a police building, so he arranged it that we meet at his office over an hour away from the police station responsible for handling my investigation. Sean was telling me that I could expect him to be an advocate above and beyond his basic obligations; he was specifically telling me when to expect a response. And thus, was telling me how to set my expectations for his role. There was never doubt in my mind that I was deserving of Sean's advocacy or a doubt in his relentless role as my advocate.

Their empathetic attention to detail was the most dependable aspect of the next five years of my life. Victims will be setting countless expectations for all aspects of life that will be met with much uncertainty – my best advice as their helper is to have them write. everything. Down. I carried a little notebook, small enough to fit in a jacket pocket, with me about everywhere. Yes, I still took notes on legal pads and within documents but having a small notebook that's "pocketable" will serve as an external brain. It gets so foggy up there...writing the important parts not only will re-enforce memory but will serve as a security blanket to remember what comes next when panic of the unknown ensues.

When you are dealing with a victim of sexual assault, it is crucial that they understand your professional role and professional obligations to their existence as a victim. This understanding should be illustrated in multiple avenues – by direct explanation of what your job title is, by clear outline of what obligations your position has to their role as victim and by support for their establishing support in the areas needed outside of your obligations. Helping them understand your specific role will not only avoid doubt or misconception down the road, but it will also help them identify for themselves the areas in which they need the most support. A victim will interact with a multitude of "talking heads" each in their one position of expertise. A victim may have trouble determining who to approach about what, and to avoid feelings of inadequacy or causing conflict seemingly by asking the wrong question, a victim may present a false sense of confidence or understanding. Heling a victim outline possible questions that they may have for each aspect of the legal system will help them identify not only aspects in need of deeper understanding, but they may also serve as a catalyst to processing their internal conflict surrounding their status as a victim.

Without a clear understanding of each of these roles their responsibilities and their place in the victim's life, it can be incredibly confusing knowing who to go to and when. This plays in with the doubt again of the victim mind that they're burdening the wrong person with the wrong information, or that they are hurting their case by some action based on misconception from social stigmas. Anyone who has achieved something truly difficult in life knows that they did not reach that goal on their own. Part of setting expectations is establishing a support system in which you can base expectations from.

LEGAL ACCOUNTABILITY

When helping a victim of sexual assault establish support systems, it's helpful to break down the overwhelming situation into categories, working backwards toward maintaining basic needs. First and foremost, an external advocate needs to be identified in a place of official power. While finding personal representation to guide a victim through legal spheres is the ideal situation, in the scenario a victim does not have a personal advocate, it is that much more important individuals within external roles operate considering their impact to victim.

Help them understand the difference between pursuing civil and criminal action. Every victim interpreter's justice differently, and thus, every victim imagines what outcome they need to heal a little differently. To some, jail time is what they view as most important in terms of vindication; others, having to register as a sex offender is a more important factor. Understanding the possible outcomes within civil and criminal pursuits may help the victim decide on one course of action over another. Perhaps they don't want to pursue criminal charges involving an official investigation and opt to solely pursue civil action. Others may see civil action as futile and only see merit in letting a criminal investigation run its course. Outside of ethical care/mandatory reporting, these decisions are the right of the victim, and as such, it's their right to make the decision given the most information they could possibly have at the time.

In order to responsibly decide on a course of action, it is essential that they understand what to expect from each. For example, understanding the role of a District Attorney (DA) will enable them to have certain expectations when interacting with the DA, what kind of questions a DA would ask and where their motivation stems for asking such questions. Understanding this motivation not only helps the victim separate the personal aspect of the situation, but it will also help them to gauge their response to give the person asking the question the most information possible. The same idea is true by understanding the role of the criminal defendant, and so forth.

FIND YOUR THREE

As we know, the transformation from victim to survivor is not instant. Even when we determine the correct step forward when considering legal needs, victims are presented with the daunting task of actually doing the work to heal. Healing from trauma is a process that does not only involve healing the damaged parts of one's mind but healing from the effect that that mental damage has on daily function. When we know the external world is secure, we are able to tune our focus into what is unsettled inside. There are three main pillars in which a victim needs to ensure that they have support – physically, psychologically, and personally.

PHYSICAL PILLAR

Regardless of the extent of physical harm during the initial instance of trauma, the physical aftershocks can be felt indefinitely. It was the beginning of 2023, when I my urologist asked a question I had not expected. I had met with a specialist at OHSU twice before e imposing this possibility. In the gentlest way he could suggest, he asked the question, "I'm so sorry to ask, but I wonder, have you experienced sexual trauma?" Dumbfounded by the realization there was a connection between my current symptoms and past abuse, I felt silly for not bringing it up before. I had been physically damaged, to the point a twenty-five-year-old has a stash of Depends in the bottom drawer.

Encourage victims to seek a relationship with a primary care provider if they don't already have one. Normalize their need to pay attention to the healing of their physical body alongside their emotional state. Suggest they seek specialists in the areas they are experiencing the most pain, be it an orthodontist or pelvic floor specialist. We will never fully understand the severity in which a victim's body internalizes abuse.

PSYCHOLOGICAL PILLAR

Every person walking this earth needs a therapist. Do you know why? Every single person walking this earth has experienced some form of trauma.

Shocker.

There are those among us still, who've experienced trauma to a degree that most will not understand. As we've already come to the agreement of the physical damage trauma brings, is it not so much more impactful when dealing with an organ there is no measurement for the degree of damage on. Our mental rigidity find itself lacking when one is in a constant state of being questioned. And because legal processes not in all a quick lane service, a victim needs to have the proper tools in place to build their mental toughness. Talking with a counselor or therapist, whatever the victim has access to allowing them the greatest ease for therapy, will ensure the victim is able to actively be present when mental clarity is demanded. It will also help them establish boundaries and maintain the ideal of expectations from different positions or structures.

PERSONAL PILLAR

While physical and psychological needs are absolutely incorporated with the person, there is a separation between the needs of the first two and the needs of this last. Ideally, your doctor has an MD. Ideally you are a therapist or counselor has some form of degree or professional certification. Here in the personal department, we look not toward professional avenues of support but the need for someone outside of a job description. I'm talking about having the specific support of a close family member of a close friend, a confidant who can walk along the side all of the crazy shitake that has and is about to happen; someone to bear witness to the fact that this victim overcame in spite of all odds. A constant, dependable voice to ground victim as they labor through the fight for survivorship as they withstand legal hailstorm.

Chances are, if you've made it thus far with me here, you're someone who cares deeply about others. You see the pain in your clients' eyes, and you wish you could erase their victimization. By making the effort to establish expectations and encourage victim to establish their own support structures, I am confident you will have established the concrete foundation needed to best enable healing. You ready, gladiator? Let's begin.

4

LEGAL SYSTEMS 101

While in high school, sixteen, my parents fostered three girls and decided to start the adoption process. By the time my graduation rolled around, four new siblings found their place in our family.. While I was quite focused on my obligations to class work and my work at the spa/floral shop in town, I was all too keen on the conflict surrounding the frankly disgusting world that is family law. Seeing that while it is preached but this system is focused on doing what is best for the child, it is abundantly clear that what is best for the child can only be done given it meets certain predetermined criteria set by individuals with no knowledge of the exact situation in which the child finds themselves. This could be said about frankly any area of law for we live in a world where circumstance matters and yet there has to be some form of consistent treatment. All that to say – I knew in the back of my mind that I was going to pursue law, but I was not going to touch family law with a ten-foot pole.

"International Transactional Corporate Law" is what I told my Jan term professor I wanted to pursue, hence why

I was taking his Law 101 class. Linfield had what was called Jan term in which the two semesters were stretched far enough apart over holiday break that there was an optional time for students to focus on a single course for the four weeks of January. Students usually filled this time with a class that had been hard to schedule prior, or they took advantage of international travel opportunities offered while faculty could take time away from typical class loads to lead expeditions. These study abroad programs were one of the reasons Linfield was at the top of my college search, but when it came time to register for classes, it didn't matter the content of others – Law 101 stared me right in the face. Over the course of those four weeks, I spent over forty hours in the Yamhill County Courthouse, observing different proceedings and developing questions to bring back to the classroom. The saying the more you know the less you understand was evident by the fact that it seemed the more I observed the more questions I developed. Alas, all of my academic pursuit and curiosity lent itself utterly useless when I found myself in the position of victim. It was as if all the knowledge I knew existed in my head was frozen, untappable, barely detectable. I had no answers, but I did know where to start with my questions. My saving grace became the confidence I had in my ability to find the answers. Had it not been for my immersion in the legal world and feeling comfortable with terminology and institutional structure, I'm not sure that I would have even known what questions to ask, let alone to begin to ask questions in general. Understanding that even the most educated victim is faced with a sense of inadequacy will help you relate to their circumstance when setting forth on their legal journey. By setting expectations of your role and the role of others, they will be able to develop and understanding of who to turn to when further understanding is required. It's impossible to expect a victim to obtain a complete legal education, Doctor of Psychology and all the medical practice necessary to heal all the damage their trauma has caused. This is why *you* enter their lives. *You* are the expert in your practice. By exposing yourself to the various fronts a victim faces and committing to a trauma informed practice, you will facilitate the greatest opportunity for healing possible. Once these expectations are set, we move towards offering a basic foundation of legal knowledge on which the victim will build from in order to make fundamental decisions.

BREAKING DOWN BUILDING BLOCKS

Trauma impacts our bodies on a biological level. Even as I had a hundred or more previous encounters with airport security, my body will always remember the experience of passing through security at the courthouse first and foremost. As primates, we may often forget, but we are animals ourselves. Every moment of life we are going through different stimuli in which we are registering different responses in different mental patterns. The more importance an event holds in our lives, the more we subconsciously collect data from our current stimuli. In our youth, we experience new encounters at a higher frequency, meaning there is more data being collected, in order to be interpreted later in life. As we get older, and find ourselves encountering more redundancy, those patterns become more of muscle memory instead of active expression. A traumatic event imposes conflicting stimuli to an environment previously deemed stable, causing those patterns to be disrupted and in turn disrupting everything reliant upon that pattern, just as a train on the tracks. If we were to extend this analogy further of our brain being the earth with a complex pattern of railroad tracks across – the earth is your prefrontal cortex. When you touch your forehead and an attempt to indicate Eureka, you are touching your prefrontal cortex. Here is your operating center your commanding voice your rational thought your decision maker. Across the earth runs a myriad of railroad lines and these represent your nervous system enabling communication. Fond on the tracks are these different patterns, boxcars filled with memories as is the hippocampus, being propelled on their track on the pace set by the amygdala. Every day that we navigate life these box cars are being filled with more memories transporting more sensory information offering the ability for our patterns to be developed with deeper context and deeper complexity. Imagine now that instead of a steam engine releasing the right amount of steam to propel it on its journey there is an imbalance of energy causing chaotic movement.

One phrase uttered more often over the past five years than any other – my mind is a mess. I'm in a constant state of standing in the middle of a train yard.

When I say my mind is a mess, I'm trying to say I feel like there are steam engines blowing in my mind and I cannot make sense of anything outside the noise. When we find ourselves in this state of confusion, we look toward those that can offer advocacy to help us calm the ensuing storm; that will help us fight through the battle within our mind. Understanding that victims exist with a multitude of demands on their attention and emotional state will help you understand what legal information is pertinent the victim understand, when. Understanding how the trauma they endured will reshape their relationship with the world enables you as advocate to facilitate obtaining understanding as a victim's journeys towards survivorship.

THIRTEEN HOURS

It was the day of the settlement conference. The entire week before I didn't move thirty feet from the toilet. My body has internalized its trauma to the point that I can ignore it most given days; But there is just sometimes in which my body overrides my mind to let it know that it is stressed beyond its capabilities. Water was coming out of both ends. These symptoms were not completely out of the ordinary, as I've dealt with daily nausea since the incident in 2019. When I describe it to people, I ask if they remember their last hangover – then ask them to image that never went away. Usually, it just lasts through the morning, nothing a tab of Zofran can't tackle. But this was one of those days, one of those weeks, nothing would subside the physical representation of my internalized dread of this day.

As we take our place in the blind drawing room, Sean jumps into action making sure that he sets the stage with the actors of the day, attorney warmups if you will. Erin seems to know every thought racing through my mind, and she begins offering a broad overview of what to expect, who was present and what would be going on in each room. She had mentioned our mediator before, but this is when she really began to talk about the Judge, Judge Jean Mauer. It wasn't until Judge Mauer entered the room that I understood the gravity of the reputation of your mediator, them being the liaison between the logical rule of law and the emotional position of a victim. She drew me this diagram illustrating the feelings of personal achievement by finding resolution and a settlement conference versus taking one's chance at trial. Even the forty-plus hours I had spent sitting in witness of courtroom proceedings could not have prepared me to understand the gravity of that situation.

The only way to understand the gravity of said situation is by experiencing it for oneself. Realistically, this is not a feasible way to prepare. Enter *you*. Your expertise combined with understanding of trauma will provide the victim with all pertinent knowledge needed in order for them to effectively take part in their own advocacy within the justice system and in the world beyond.

VOCAB

One of the best ways to empower a victim is to instill confidence through education surrounding legal terminology in which they are engaging. Before being able to understand the institutional structure of the justice system, it is important to have a basic understanding of what terms are used, how they relate to the victim's experience and when to expect them to arise. In the back of this book, you will find a glossary containing 100+ terms a victim should be made aware of as they begin their legal journey. Twice as many unknown vocabulary words will arise over the course of their trek and half of the terms originally reviewed will be remembered when they actually arise; but think of vocabulary words as seeds planted – the earlier the seed is planted the more time it has to develop and grow, and the sooner our victim is exposed to the terminology of the justice system the sooner they can start identifying gaps in which they need to expand their understanding.

CRIMINAL SYSTEM

When engaging in criminal pursuits it's important for the victim to understand that this is the state pursuing accountability toward the wrongdoings of an individual – in criminal proceedings, well there is much effort to provide avenues for restitution and healing, the victim is involved as a witness. It is important that a victim understands what outcomes are possible within criminal proceedings to avoid feelings of failure in the case of a less than favorable outcome. Even navigating the checkpoints of criminal efforts can feel sterile to the person that suffers the most from the incident occurring. Criminal proceedings can make a victim feel as though the punishment toward someone's wrongful actions is more important than finding ways to make the victim whole. It's also poor important to note that specific legal proceedings can vary from state to state either as minimally as a different name for the same proceeding or for a proceeding in one state that is mandatory to be optional in another. Again, this serves to exemplify the importance for those in a victim's life to be honest in their area of expertise and offer the support of a victim as they build their legal knowledge.

REPORT

Filing an official police report outlining one's trauma probably the single greatest for challenge for a victim, because it is at this point that they have to stand on their courage alone to share the truth of what happened. Filing an official report brings a flood of emotions even after the confidence to make such a statement as made. By nature of reporting and opening an investigation there suggests there is an element of doubt to the victims truth. Help a victim understand how this is the initiating step, what this action sets into motion.

INVESTIGATION

Once an investigation is opened, the victim will spend weeks to months in a state of constant questioning. They need to understand that the purpose of the investigation is to collect as much information relating to the incident as possible so that all involved in the conversation surrounding the incident can know that they are operating with all possible information. It's important that you help the victim understand the asking questions does not always imply doubt but can offers the ability for unbiased confirmation. Walk them through when they may be asked to give statements, who is performing the investigation and what investigators are analyzing when gathering statements.

CASE ENTRY

After enough information has been collected to present a case to the District Attorney, it must be reviewed by the legal staff to determine if there is enough information to pursue criminal charges. It's important for a victim to understand that the review is not about if they believe the incident occurred or if charges should be pursued, this stage is merely about determining if enough evidence exists for the case to proceed to trial. It is important a victim understand what goes into the decision-making process of the DA, what factors are evaluated and what aspects are important moving forward.

ARRAIGNMENT

Once a case has been entered and a suspect charged, the arrangement is held for the accused to enter a plea regarding the charges against them. The victims may expect more specific or factual information to be discussed but should understand that this is simply an opportunity for the accused to make their initial appearance and iron out any functional aspects of the case.

PRELIMINARY HEARING/ GRAND JURY

In the federal system, indictment by grand jury is mandatory to pursue accountability for a crime. States have the option to require indictments, and when no such requirement is made, the accused goes to the process of the preliminary hearing. Oftentimes, one incident can be broken down into several criminal actions, and without understanding individual charges can impact the indictment, a victim can find themselves feeling lost in between the lines of legal terminology. It is vital a victim understands why specific charges are brought, how each may be treated differently. Guide the victim through developing the vocabulary to outline why the specific charges impact their identity as victim and what their view of retribution might be.

TRIAL

Preferably, and if at all possible, it is favorable for a victim to avoid having to endure the humiliating process of trial – again being placed on a stage to be combed over with a microscope. Avenues for finding resolution can be found and attempts to hold settlement conferences, pretrial motions, or straight forward mediation. When all these avenues have failed, trial begins. Just as in the beginning, it is important to remind the victim that the goal of these proceedings is to identify if the accused individual conducted the accused actions beyond a reasonable doubt. The burden of proof, or the party responsible proving their side, lies with the state demonstrating enough evidence to deter any doubt of the accused actions.

CIVIL PROCEEDINGS

Complaint Filed

Contrary to the burden of proof in criminal proceedings, in civil proceedings, the plaintiff (or in our case the victim) is responsible for proving harm was committed based on a preponderance of the evidence, i.e. more likely than not put plainly, if there were a hundred people in the room, the victim need only convince fifty-one of those people that the accused is responsible for their trauma. It is vital for the victim to understand that the structure of civil suits is to determine if the accused parley should be held accountable for the alleged action. Civil pursuits are not to determine responsibility nor hold accountability in a criminal sense. This is why the need for two different structures exist but why issues regarding sexual assaults can often seem confusing; both courses of action seem interconnected and dependent on the other. The complaint filed in a civil proceeding typically includes an outline of the nature of the complaint, parties involved, jurisdictional aspects, applicable law, facts of the case and claims for relief – all aspects of which a victim may feel overwhelmed by reading comprehensively for the first time. It's important for the victim to understand that the original complaint filed often encompasses broad information or working guesstimations of which specific numbers will be proved when they become pertinent.

Answer Filed

The accused party now turned defendant must file an answer to the complaint made. It is important for the victim to know here that this is the accused's first response toward the claims made about them. Just as in the original complaint where broad or general information is used before specific information is gathered, the response of the defendant may make a victim panic, even if denial was fully expected. Reading line by line responses toward why everything you said or claimed to be true is wrong can cause great doubt in a victim's decision to pursue account-ability. It is important for the victim to understand that denial should be anticipated, Least the accused walking to the police station and surrender themselves! If the accused was to respond and their answer and say, "Yes, all this is true, nothing to deny or disagree with here," there would be no point to a trial. A victim must understand that this is simply the place from which we identify what facts are accepted as true on both sides and where lies disagreement and thus, where lies the debate.

Judge Reviews

Just as in an arrangement for criminal proceedings, this is a time in which the judge will outline logistics of the case. It is important that a victim understands this is not the time for the judge to weigh in on the facts at hand but to merely ensure all the players have set the board game correctly and intend to conduct a fair game.

Phase of Discovery

This is when the details are ironed. During this time ranging from months to years, a victim will endure a roller coaster of emotion. headway is made through the exchange of critical information to the case, perhaps new information is brought to light by private investigators. But while all this happens within the legal halls the victim will only feel better about their everyday surroundings. It is important that a victim understand that care is being taken towards their legal proceedings and it is their responsibility to focus on life outside the courtroom.

Settlement Conference

Here is when a mediator is engaged to determine if resolution can be found between the two parties before advancement to trial. Here it is important that the victim understands that by engaging with a settlement conference, they are engaging with the intent to find compromise in expectations of accountability and probable convincible outcome They are never expected to compromise on their position as victim.

Trial

As with the burden of proof explained earlier, civil trial is aimed at identifying if the accused party more likely than not committed the crime. While this seems an easy threshold to reach for any victim bearing witness to the reality of the situation, but the reality in the world of law is that there is never such a guaranteed outcome. It is important for the victim to understand that this trial here is not to determine if the accused party is guilty, but if they should be responsible for the impact toward you the victim based on presented evidence.

GODSPEED

Just as you endured orientation before your first day at the office, or perhaps thinking back to your internship orientation pre-grad, while sitting in the presentation itself felt endless, you probably walked away with confidence in the path ahead because you had been given expectations. You had even the slightest vision of what was to come and the tools you would need to succeed. Once you are able to set expectations and offer a basic foundation of legal understanding, your victimized client will be ready and able to take part alongside your own efforts of advocacy for their position. This is how we lead victims out of their dark world of victimization and toward their life as survivor.

Now that we know the path, now that we have the necessary tools – the hard work actually begins.

5

AND SO, IT BEGINS

Regardless of a victim's decision pursuing criminal and/or civil action, there are a multitude of steps within each step that causes the legal process to feel very lengthy. In the first twenty-four hours after an incident happens, a victim will go through an internal battle convincing themselves that the trauma actually occurred, and that pursuing official accountability is the correct course of action. Once the victim has reached the place they have reported, found external advocacy, and identified their legal course of action, it may seem to them far too much time has already passed since the incident took place. There is often frustration stemming from misconceptions about timelines or sequence of events; thus, having expectations set given an understanding of different courses of action will best enable healing once proceedings have begun.

EXPOSED

December 10, 2019. My attorneys filed my lawsuit against Jubb and Linfield on December 10 at 11:49 in the morning. At 6:22 that evening, an article in The Oregonian had been published outlining all public details that, prior to this point, had remained intimate knowledge of myself and those involved with the investigation. By 6:00 am the next morning, I had received messages from over one hundred individuals commenting on their shock toward the situation. More than twenty of those individuals expressed some form of sexual trauma that was undermined or neglected by Linfield administration. Over the course of the next few months, I would come to hear near a hundred stories by accounts of individuals who felt traumatized by their institution's response to their traumatic event, many of whom have shared part in my own survivor's journey. Little did I know sharing common trauma would lead me to find both my hairdresser and my CPA!

But back to the topic at hand. of press. The news thrives on emotional stories – emotion is often rooted in conflict, struggle, disagreement, and traumatic events. Be it if you live in a small town where every sneeze by your neighbor is met with a blessed you from the next or be it you live in a large community where your existence feels is no more important than that of a worker ant, any victim should feel prepared for their account of truth to be magnified and dissected. There will be those who's responsibility it is to magnify in pursuit of justice, and there will be those who choose to magnify if not only for their own twisted fulfillment. It is important to understand that as victims, we want to shy away from putting ourselves into a position to be criticized. Finding the strength to encounter criticism is the only way and which we can create the opportunity to also receive validation – just maybe, through finding your courage to speak, another witnessing your actions will find the same courage within themselves to do the same.

Aside from preparing for a flood of criticism, there are other aspects of one's daily life that should be considered, if not only to have a game plan ready that is never used.

TIPS AND TRICKS

Media capitalizes on emotion because emotion is what most often what motivates our actions. When loved ones, friends, acquaintances, coworkers and even strangers learn of another's victim status, the immediate, emotional response is to make their awareness of the situation known. Help the victim develop general responses to use when asked about aspects of the case. Having clear expectations for what should be discussed with whom will not only give the victim confidence of their privacy but will also reinforce they are not expected to forever remain silent. Help them understand the difference between confiding in their person, counselor, or life coach and an acceptable response for those whom the care but don't want to share intimate information. A victim may feel overwhelmed with the inquisitive nature of those around them and thus it's imperative that they find mechanisms not only for navigating conversations, but also for handling the stress that is brought by such visibility. Remember, the victim is navigating this oddly floating existence in the legal world for years. For years, the victim is going to have random weeks in which they will keep facts of the traumatic incident at the forefront of their mind; then, suddenly, months that they are expected to go about life as if there isn't a guillotine hanging above their head. This is why the support systems are so important. A victim cannot be expected to survive alone in this purgatory; their pillars of support are critical to their survival.

After establishing their support pillars, victims should also give themselves grace in accepting this process of navigating the legal system and finding one's survivor skills happens slowly over time. Survival skills are learned through navigating triggering events, sometimes very poorly at first, but their own method for mental toughness will be found. Be it through trial and error, or a suggestion from someone who's shared the same struggle, remind the victim their method for healing is as unique as their trauma is – none of us share the exact same pain, but we all share common pursuit of healing.

Listing potential triggers victims may encounter would be an exercise in futility; thus, there is no way for me to predict what triggering stimuli your client may find most challenging about navigating daily life suffering from the impact of their trauma. There are, however, commonly shared themes in those living in the wake of post-traumatic stress. Approaching external stressors with the understanding of the impact of trauma will enable the victim to not only treat symptoms of their stress, but it will also help them process why such events are happening in hopes of reducing future recurrence.

If it wasn't obvious by my childhood or my decisions throughout college, I'm a control freak. I've been a control freak ever since I experienced control being stripped away from my thirteen-year-old self. Needless to say, living the life of a victim, you are all too aware that you have zero control over what happens to you; the only control you have in life is the control you have over your response. Here is where I find my cleansing breath. When I am faced with a painful trigger, a painful experience, a painful encounter – I exhale all the pain with my breath. As I inhale, I fill my lungs with new life, fresh encouragement, still energy. Again, I exhale the fear pain causes with intention; I relish my inhale with renewed focus. My breath is my control over life.

Each victim will develop their own physical sense of security, usually stemming from the nature of their insecurities. Victims should be prepared with tools to navigate stress in different public settings in the event their stress sends them into an episode of distress. I remember walking through a Safeway back in 2019, a store no one would have recognized me. While deciding on toilet paper, a gentleman walked past I thought I recognized from Linfield. I remember leaning against the toilet paper rolls, trying to catch my breath. I remember telling myself I wasn't allowed to break down in the store, to hold it together till I got to the car. I remember feeling, not just seeing, stars surround me as I ultimately abandon my basket and fled. That was the day I started wearing my hats.

There are many ways a victim may incorporate elements of security into their wardrobe. Wear a large, brimmed hat or baseball cap, somewhat serving as blinders against the outside world and giving you a sense of control over what happens under the brim. Wear an oversized scarf that can be flattened and wrapped around you as a shall or thin blanket, giving you an invisible hug when one needs to feel a sense of security. Find a fabric that really feels good against your skin and wear it whenever you may engage with triggering situations. Wear shoes that make you feel grounded and confident, even if they are heals.

In the event of a public panic attack – If at all possible, find a wall or something stationary to physically press yourself up against. This will ground you and give your subconscious a sense of permanence, security. If no wall is to be found, look for a permanent object such as a tree, a shelf, post, or even a person with you. Try pressing your thumb fingernail against the tip of each of your index fingers, bringing your awareness away from the stressful environment and toward the physical sensation you're experiencing on your hand.

Channel your inner Clark Kent by standing straight with your arms placed on your hips. Press your chest out and with each breath channel your inner superhero. This power stance does more than remind us of our power, but it creates lots of space in one's lungs allowing for greater oxygen flow. Countdown, like we did in the beginning of Chapter 2. Ask yourself, what are five things that I can see? What are four things that I can physically feel? What are three sounds that I hear? What are two smells in the air? What is one thing I taste? Asking yourself these questions can bring one center focus back on the breath and minimize the noise of the outside world.

Developing skills to minimize negative impact of the external world, while difficult, is much easier than helping a victim navigate the impact trauma will have to their physical health. Victims should be strongly encouraged to maintain a relationship with their primary physician, but they may have to develop strategies to mitigate daily impact through trial and error. If experiencing perpetual nausea due to stress/PTSD, there are many possible modes of relief, besides prescription medication. Carry alcohol swabs and use them like smelling salts when they feel an episode coming on. Stash Pepto Bismol or Tums, their antiacid of choice really, in chewable forms, everywhere. Keep small packets of crackers, like individual Biscoff packets (yes, I know, they're really a cookie), available for when they need to take meds or simply curb nausea due when they can't stomach anything else. Fill XL socks with barley or rice, even adding dried lavender or essential oils, so that when they're microwaved, they create a warm pack to place on their stomach, soothing with heat and scent.

Sometimes, a victim's body indicates the stress it's experiencing through strange skin reactions. Encourage the victim to know their brands, carry travel sized toiletry containers filled with the lotion and hand sanitizer products they know won't cause reactions. If they can get away with it practically, or fashionably, wear gloves to minimize interaction with the outside world. Wear loose fitting clothing that covers their irritated areas...out of sight, out of mind. If they are going to try a new product, make sure they do so when they do not have upcoming important dates on the calendar! Always give yourself a week between anything new being added to your life and any important event.

Those suffering the physical impact of sexual assault may find new pain associated with intimate areas. Pain isn't always immediate after one's initial assault. Sometimes, the damage done takes time to be made visible. Incontinence issues are commonly faced and shouldn't be thought of differently than another symptom of trauma. Learn Mind over matter – learn the power of manifesting what you want to happen. You will make it to the toilet. You don't need to pee. You are in control. Don't diss the Depends – sometimes it is more important to feel confident against physical embarrassment than it is to feel embarrassed by what people cannot see.

Wear darker, looser fitting clothing that won't show extra bulk or odd lines. Understand your bladder is controlled by muscles, your muscles were injured and deserve their own rehabilitation. See a pelvic floor specialist who can develop a physical therapy regiment around your specific needs.

If you ask your victimized client but not one question every day, it should be this: "How did you sleep?" Sleep may be the single most important aspect of the healing process for many reasons, but most pertinent to this book is the simple fact that trauma victims don't sleep. Many find methods of falling asleep regularly, many have worked through their trauma to find their survivor identity and thus, can find sleep. But dare I make such a claim, even the victim who falls asleep naturally will encounter some level of sleep disruption.

Sleep is essential to the healing process. Struggling to sleep will lead to more negative impact than can truly be understood. When a victim doesn't sleep, they enter the next day restless. This weakens their emotional fortitude and sets a stage for frustration. When one escapes to their bed after a frustrating day, they are less likely to fall asleep in a timely manner. This turns to another night without sleep, navigating another day with pent frustration. So. The cycle continues. Encourage the victim not to judge themselves for not being able to fall asleep/stay asleep. Tell them to learn their body's natural circadian rhythm and lean into the cycle. When they find themselves awake, get out of bed. If it's the middle of the night, rotate through low-energy demanding activities such as reading, journaling, or crafting. This will reinforce that when their body is horizontal in its bed, it should be programmed to sleep. Coach them to structure their night so that you anticipate midnight attention; try structuring the night so that they have two sleeps, giving themselves permission in the middle to capitalize on their body's natural energy when present.

If absolutely no sleep will come, suggest they find ways

to offer rest. Suggest they give themself a set period of time in bed. Seemingly in contradiction to the rule "Only sleeping bodies in bed," it is important that if sleep is not coming naturally, that they give their body the space to rest as though it was sleeping. Be it only for an hour or two, coaching them to lay in bed and rest, even without sleep, will allow your body some of the reset needed to process emotion and develop healing.

Navigating the life as a victim of sexual assault will be a lifelong practice, but helping the victim establish tools to approach the effect trauma has in their life will enable them to take ownership over.

6

WHILE AT SEA

ALIEN DAYS

It was the Alien Days Parade, May 2022. The sleepy town that like home to Linfield College had another claim to fame; One of the country's most popular UFO festivals, second only to that of its sister festival in Roswell, New Mexico. Instigated to honor the first and the most credible UFO documentation in the country, today the McMinnville UFO Festival was a highly anticipated week in full of exploring all things extraterrestrial. I will always be among the first to embrace the quirky and even as I have long avoided large gatherings, the UFO festival was one large scale activity I look forward to anticipating during my early years in Oregon. Since my assault on February 15th of 2019, I have been paralyzed at the thought of being in a crowded room up until this point in May of '22, I had not navigated any large congregation of people. Yes, though there have been airports, and the paralyzing sound of those metal detectors, but I had not been a situation in which I was pressed against other people, even in an outdoor space. I was there with my family, even if they were not my blood, for the Kiffs had adopted me as their own since our first interaction. Both parents were there, Laurie and Joel, as well as one of the brothers, Robin, the sister, Erin, her husband, Tyler, and their daughter, McKenzie. Eventually, I was separated from the group and, in effort to find my way back to our corridor, found myself swimming in the sea of people. Up until this point, my hat had served to offer my world of security admits the swirling crowd, but upon seeing a member of the Linfield administration that in all reality I had wish would have been smithed where she stood, I lost my ability to retain my composure and had quite the panic attack. Calling Robin, he immediately sensed my state. Calmly, he kept repeating that I was going to be okay, to focus on my breath, whilst guiding me toward the rendezvous point. Once I reached the group, the parade had ended so we started retracing our steps back toward the car. The natural way to navigate a large group through a crowd is by single file line; instead, they seemed to form a blockade around me, shielding me from the stress of the crowd. Without speaking a word of my distress, they sensed a simple movement on their part would create an environment enabling me to relax. Their behavior wasn't even obvious at the time; it was later when talking to Robin that this all became clear. You see, Robin had intimate knowledge of my fear of crowds and the reason for such fear. While the rest of his family knew that I struggled with crowds in some way, they did not have intimate knowledge of why or to what extent. All they had to know was that I needed extra protection, and it didn't matter why or who I ultimately was: they came around me because they understood the need to support.

NAVIGATING DAILY TASKS

Have you ever taken an extended trip abroad? Do you remember driving for the first time? Sitting in your car, putting it in reverse, flipping the turn signal? Perhaps you went carless for a time or needed use of a rental; whatever the reason, if you think hard enough, you can relate to a situation in which you resumed a task once thought of as second nature. Most all of us would like to admit we resumed driving without the slightest hiccup; however, I feel most of us made some error, however slight. If nothing more, you feel the feeling of things being "normal" again because you experienced feeling that things were not, "normal."

Resuming daily tasks in the wake of a traumatic event can often feel like this – instead – you never feel as though things are "normal' again. You know they *should* feel normal, but you're stuck driving on the wrong side of the road and you can't switch back.

During a traumatic event, your mind is intensifying its memory. Think of flare systems, alert notices, being associated with the stimuli present in the painful experience. From now on, your body will sense these alerts and prevent you from experiencing something as painful ever again. Or so it believes. Think back to the security checkpoint. There's no rational reason that I should associate putting my wallet and shoes into a plastic bin as a reason to start panicking and losing my breath. But because that was the situation I was in moments before seeing my assaulter for the first time in four years, I associate those actions and that environment with that panicked state.

Understanding that victims will experience stimuli as

they perform everyday duties will help those in the victim's life understand how they are best able to lend support. Tasks as simple as standing in line at the post office can offer complication if, by chance, another individual waiting in the same line resembles the victim's perpetrator. Coping mechanisms to help the victim focus on the present are essential in navigating unexpected triggers. Outside of coping with panicked moments, a victims three pillars of support should function as a unit to ensure the victim is on the best path towards healing, not simply coping.

PHYSICAL PILLAR

The importance of establishing a relationship with a medical professional was mentioned when setting expectations. Here again, it's importance is reiterated. Your primary care physician should act as the funnel through which all your medical needs are directed. Outside of immediate physical assistance, they will be able to help direct you toward counseling services and any specialized professionals surrounding your specific traumatic needs. If you encourage the victim to see no other specialist, I recommend every victim of sexual assault visit with a pelvic floor specialist. Paying attention to areas in which we harbor the most pain and avoidance takes strength. It is often the mindset of a victim to feel as though If they don't accept their current reality that they may always live in that mindset of a victim. It is possible to accept you have been victimized and also accept that you do not live the life of a victim. Oftentimes, when we are traumatized in one area, we do everything that we can to build a shell protecting that area from being harmed again. It took nearly a month of appointments of my specialist simply placing her hand over my belly button before I was comfortable with any further touch. Paying attention to the area I had subconsciously guarded as the source of all my pain did not only bring medical benefit, but it brought a new ability to pay attention toward the pain that could not be seen in a physical sense.

PSYCHOLOGICAL PILLAR

While ensuring the correct medical professionals are guiding you through physical healing, we know that the largest portion of the trauma iceberg that is that found beneath the surface. Damage from a traumatic event does not only stem from the actions of the perpetrator but can also stem from how the circumstance of our trauma happening is addressed and handled. As is exemplified with institutional betrayal, one can suffer compounded trauma when their story of abuse is put on a pedestal to be analyzed, giving contradicting parties opportunity to minimize the victims experience. The nature of a lawsuit is to put actions in the light to find truth and responsibility, and as such, a victim is put into a place where it feels as though anyone interacting with this situation is either for you or against you. A victim will need to develop tactics for isolating their victim mentality from present reality. The best mental health professionals will act as a guide for the victim to process their own trauma; given in them the tools needed, walking alongside the digging and sorting of the painful past, offering assistance sorting and processing to proceed forward anew. It is not because of them the victim finds healing; they are there to show them how to heal themselves.

The position of someone who is completely detached from the implications toward one's life, but yet, is filled with great empathy and care for the existence of said individual is an utterly underappreciated position. Given this stance, a person is able to offer insight only be seen from an outsider's perspective, without being directly impacted from sharing such position. Just like every mom needs someone else to tell their child that they should probably take a shower sooner than later, or perhaps taking that personal finance class wouldn't be such a bad idea. No one wants to listen to their mother. When an outside voice offers the same guidance that we know we would get from a loved one, it offers some validity to the stance that that person isn't saying such simply because they love you. Outside perspective is vital to the victims' experience, not only validating their existence as a victim, but in helping them express challenges faced that would express to family be humiliating or demeaning. This place of external insight offers the ability for honest conversation well understanding its protected security.

PERSONAL PILLAR

Ensuring that you have a person in your corner that is there for nothing other than personal support of the victim is the third pillar to successful healing. This may seem like such an obvious statement to make, I've made it before; but as I've stated a million times over, it is the essence of navigating the legal system as a victim of sexual assault to be doubted. The victim will need a personal cheerleader that can be there to scream their self-worth, echoing the words of the medical professionals and legal staff. *You are not a burden.* This person can be a mother, a father, sister, brother, classmate, mentor, coworker – anyone the victim finds solace in that is in a place of consistency in their life. Ideally when we think of people that are there through thick and thin, we think of family. Family is not always blood. We create our families; we are born to our relatives. A victim will need to rely on their family even when they cannot vocalize help, and often this help is best received in the form of simply knowing that they are surrounded by people who love them.

ALL THAT, AND A POT OF CHILI

We've all been told how important it is that we choose our partners with care. When you're young, you feel this advice is given as a means to control tour every action, just another way for someone to tell you what to do and how it should be done. In my pursuit of advocacy, I met a man whose son quickly stole my heart. In the midst of a pandemic, he needed education, and I needed a greater purpose. We both needed love. I ignored every red flag that waved me down, rationalizing them away with my great capacity to love. Victims of sexual assault will forever seek safety and security; this is why having established support systems is imperative to their healing. When they feel the need to search for and establish those support systems on their own, they risk making judgements influenced by our most primitive nature – find safety.

The first moment I knew I had made a grave error was when a CPAP machine was hurled through the air. I temporarily move out the next week, but we ultimately decided to remain together for the sake of the son. I had made a commitment to them both, and the father agreed to begin counseling. At first, relationship was better than ever, until all the sudden it wasn't. Earlier that day, he requested I make his favorite chili. He left, only to return in fuss, erupted for a reason I frankly don't even remember, and left again. I thought he was staying at the second apartment we had at the time, thinking it was responsible of him to cool off before saying or doing something catastrophic.

He chose the catastrophic.

As my insomniac existence is everlasting, I was awake around 3:00 a.m. when I heard voices in the kitchen. My only explanation was that he came home and turned on the TV, otherwise I was not alone in the house all day as I had thought...I walked out to the kitchen to find him home, sure enough, but home with a woman and the pot of chili I had made in-between her legs as she sat on my kitchen island, my husband standing in front of her, spoon feeding her, the chili. My response? "How does it taste?" What else could be said when someone makes hard decision for you?

We were officially divorced two months later.

Fast forward to Spring 2023. I was cleaning out an old email inbox. This was the email associated to my LinkedIn account, and post the February 15th incident, I had removed myself from nearly all social spheres, especially social media. In my Gmail inbox, I had received a notification for this message:

"Hi AnnaMarie. I want to first tell you that I am so sorry for what has happened to you! No women should ever have to go through anything like this but it's amazing how strong you've been to standup for yourself! I secondly want to admit that Pam is not my real name. I have a lot to lose by telling you this info but I just couldn't not tell you. I don't want to be the bearer of bad news; however, this info was completely shocking and disgusting to me. James Edwards contacted David Jubb's attorney to try and get paid for his testimony against you. He claims he has text messages, recorded phone conversations, videos, and audio recordings of sexual proclivities. He claimed he has information about your past that would help Jubb's case.

Also, he doesn't believe that you were opposed to something sexual happening with Jubb. I am so sorry to tell you all of this, I was just astounded someone, let alone a partner would behave this way. Stay strong girl!"

Advocating for victims of sexual violence requires empathetic care extended to all areas of their life. Sometimes, showing care requires posing difficult questions. Helping a victim examine the health of their existing or arising personal relationships can be tedious, obviously there are certain actors in a victims experience more equipped to engage in such conversations than others. Pose questions in a manner that makes it clear you are simply helping the victim think out loud; you are presenting them with a mirror in which they can most clearly see themselves to make the right decision. Your love and support of them remains beyond their choice.

DOREECE

When you spend a lot of your time as a victim discussing matters that carry such weight in the courtroom, it's hard to feel that simpler tasks held any importance. This is compounded by not being able to talk about the majority of specifics when it comes to aspects of your case, a victim can find themself living in a state of isolation for years on end. Instead of allowing the victim to perpetuate their isolation, make a point to identify the advantages of their current living situation. If the victim already lives with family or roommate, encourage them to vocalize their need for support surrounding the areas that they specifically engage with the most challenge. If a victim lives by themselves, it is important that you help them establish built in reinforcements for when they need help but are unable to vocalize. This may look like starting a weekly friend gathering, allowing a non-direct way for friends to gauge the well-being of the victim. This may look like asking a mentor for monthly coffee check-ins where the victim can vocalize current frustrations of the case. Whomever it may be help the victim identify the one person, two, if necessary, that will be the third cornerstone on their journey of healing.

This personal pillar of support can offer stability in a victim's life beyond navigating daily tasks, they may offer stability when insight toward life decision is needed and difficult to process when a large portion of the victim's life seems unstable and ever changing. Existing in this state of limbo can cause a victim to feel that decisions regarding school occupation or even romance can be difficult to determine what the victims' personal feelings are and what is what feelings are rooted in a nature of anxiety caused by existence in the justice system.

When retreating from the wounds of the world, my personal pillar put a book in my hands.

"What is your best discovery?" asked the mole.

"That I'm enough as I am," said the boy.

"I've realized why we are here," whispered the boy.

"For cake?" asked the mole.

"To love," said the boy.

"And be loved," said the horse.

"What do we do when our hearts hurt?" asked the boy.

"We wrap them with friendship, shared tears and time, till they wake hopeful and happy again."

"Do you have any other advice?" asked the boy.

"Don't measure how valuable you are by the way you are treated," said the horse.

"Always remember you matter, you are important, and you are loved, and you bring to this world things no one else can."

These pages in my copy of *The Boy, The Mole, The Fox and The Horse* are tear stained; a simple passage that served to quiet the dark voices of doubt echoing in a victim's mind. When you find yourself a victim of sexual assault, it's easy to believe the lie that you were chosen because you're not worth anything. Living life as a victim of sexual assault means actively choosing every day to reinforce yourself worth; toto remind yourself daily that the worth of your existence isn't determined by others.

FINANCIAL GUIDANCE

An overlooked area a victim will need specific guidance is that of their financial needs. As a victim, you exist in a primitive state, worrying about basic necessities and fearing something bad is going to happen at any given second. This prolonged state of survival it can make financial decisions feel incredibly heavy, be it deciding how to spend five hundred dollars or five million. Establishing a relationship with someone in a place of financial advice is essential from an early point in a victim's legal process. This financial advice should not only be given from the position of someone only focused on thy financial best core strategy, but advice given to the victim with their unique situation in mind. Financial advisors may not always give the best financial advice, and family members may not always have your best interest in mind. The best advice stems from seeking balanced counsel. It's vital to find a balance between the insight of professionals, as we must understand that their voice comes from a place of expertise within their specific field, and the personal input from the people that we love. only stem after the cornerstones of support structure have been established.

ELECTRONIC COMMUNICATIONS

There will be times when your victimized clients interact with the need to communicate, be it through e-mail text message or phone call, and quick insight from one's attorney is not always possible. Establishing the proper protocol of when and whom with texting or phone calls are appropriate will ensure the victim has no barriers in reaching out for help. Perhaps the victim will be in a medical waiting room filling out paperwork only confronted with panic, thinking that if they circle or check the box for depression or anxiety that they will complicating how their mental state is argued in the courtroom. Perhaps a victim finds himself crippled when faced with a conversation surrounding medication. Maybe a victim will be in the grocery store only to find that the checker that they got in line for reminds them of their abuser. Perhaps a conversation that arises in class incorporates specific terms that trigger moments before trauma. Understanding that victims will experience triggering stimuli in every area of their life will help those surrounding them understand how they can best lend support.

JUST KEEP SWIMMING

It's also vital to ensure that the victim understands that life should not stand still simply because they feel their case does. A victim can feel as though there is no need to focus on achieving professional goals or pursuing academic achievement cannot fully be given energy until after the legal situation is resolved. This feeling can stem from a victim's mindset that they doubt the state that they are in as a victim and believe that finding resolution in the legal system will offer their victim status validity. When a victim equates the end of a legal process with the end of their constant state of stress or doubt, this sets a victim up to feel personal inadequacy when the end of their legal journey is realized, and it becomes evident that their trauma still exists. Establishing these pillars of support will help remind the victim their life is worthy of being lived beyond the status of their abuser's conviction. They alone determine their ability to become a survivor. With the proper people and places of support a victim will be able to continue through graduation, they'll be able to get the promotion they wouldn't have thought prior, they'll even be able to navigate new romance with the confidence. Confidence that their victim status is not causing them to live frozen in their victim mentality.

7

RESOLUTION?

I f I was to honestly answer my attorneys when asked what I viewed as a just outcome, I would have asked for something less politically correct. Any victim wants their perpetrator to experience exactly what was done to them – if not worse for the sake of their organic desire in the first place. What did I really want done to Jubb? I wanted him to know what it was like to feel vulnerable at the hand of another; I wanted him to know what it is like to feel trapped by voices telling him he was worthless; I wanted him to truly consider himself nothing but a means to another's arousal. How could the justice system be expected to pose such punishment? How do you quantify such mind-fuckery?

The reality of finding resolution is that there is never a single victor. T true resolution is found in what is the best outcome possible given the factors at hand. Be it in civil or criminal pursuits, it is imperative that the victim remain honest to oneself about their capabilities moving past the traumatic event outside of the end result of legal proceedings. Accepting reality as it is does not always mean condoning its existence as good – we sometimes merely need to find contentment where we are placed and accept what which is.

CIVIL RESOLUTION

If you've never experienced courtroom proceedings for yourself, your mind may envision the beginning of *12 Angry Men*. Death and life hang in the balance; the weight of the moment felt beyond the walls of the office they sat, into the night for which long they deliberated. It would be nice if at the end of a multi-year battle there was some gravitas once the end was reached.

Resolution in the civil world feels much less than satisfactory than what is probably imagined when a victim is picturing their day of justice. When a civil case is settled, it can feel as though years of sacrificed health and wellbeing were in vain, regardless of what final judgment is made. If we all think back to kids on the playground, when we felt offended or wronged another, we we're taught the demonstration of remorse was the sign of a truly apologetic heart; seemingly, once the words "I'm sorry" were uttered, it was back to playing tag as usual. If there were only a way to force perpetrators to simply state their regret and if a victim could know that it was sincere, we may be able to live in a society where healing from sexual abuse is actually possible. But because of the nature of sexual crimes, victims will always live in a mindset that what was done to them does it matter to anyone else because it will never matter to the person who committed such action. This is where our conversation surrounding expectations carries great weight. If a victim is guided through recognizing what their priorities in terms of justice are, they will be able to more objectively see their position of success when entering into the space that compromises are made. Ensure the victim is considering their immediate needs as well as long term implications of such resolution. Help the victim play-out the next five, ten, twenty years post resolution in order to help them vocalize their priorities. Often, the priorities a victim vocalizes during the onset of legal pursuits may evolve as the case evolves over time. By encouraging the victim to be understanding and involved with their own advocacy, you can best ensure they are accurately reflecting their needs once official resolution is signed.

CRIMINAL CONCLUSION

December 10th, my suit against Linfield became public through an article released in the Oregonian. Eight days later I received the message I had been waiting for the past ten months. I told myself when my incident with Jubb occurred, there was no way a man was able to act that way without developing such confidence through practice. I had heard Jubb had other victims, I simply hadn't spoken to any myself. It wasn't until I received this call in December that I had confirmation firsthand that this was indeed the same man that he had assaulted her and other friends that night. She recounted her experience on the evening of Jubb's abuse. It was eerie to hear such a different circumstance described but to recognize such similar behavior and obvious manipulation.

At Jubb's indictment, he was charged with one felony account of first-degree sexual assault and seven misdemeanor accounts of third degree sexual assault. It was important to me that there be at least one charge for every victim I had knowledge. Upon the day of his sentencing, Jubb managed to negate accountability of the felony charge and five misdemeanor charges. Jubb pleaded no contest to two of the misdemeanors counts, one of them on my behalf and another of an anonymous victim. Helping a victim understand the reality of the legal system will enable them to make decisions that will reflect their need for healing and the best way possible. Having a realistic perspective of what is possible through the legal system in terms of justice will prevent them from placing the weight of their healing upon specific outcomes. Each victim must find their own motivation outside a simple search for justice. For myself, I was motivated to be the last individual victimized by a then seventy-one-year-old man who had spent a lifetime grabbing whatever pussy was desired. The outcome will never be objectively just. Jail time may be traded for extended probation; registering as a sex offender may be forfeited to encourage the perpetrator to enter a specific plea on a different account. Ensuring that the victim establishes an understanding surrounding a situation deemed at making them feel as a commodity will enable them to be more involved in the process itself and minimize feelings of insignificance. By setting realistic expectations for what is possible at sentencing a victim will be able to advocate for their needs when asked for input by the DA as to what they deem most important. At sentencing a victim is given the right to make an impact statement, vocalizing whatever they need to directly vocalize to their perpetrator to find some kind of conclusion in the legal process.

Despite the outcome of criminal proceedings, victims are given the opportunity to make an impact statement directed towards their abuser. This platform can be a cathartic opportunity to address the very individual the victim often spends the majority of their time addressing internally. Being provided an opportunity to publicly offer a statement gives the victim opportunity to find their own sense of closure. There is a long process of healing in the aftermath of such a gruesome battle; but leaving one's resentment in their status as victim is the best place to start.

VICTIM IMPACT

When at criminal sentencing, victims are offered the opportunity to make an impact statement. This provides an opportunity for direct confrontation without the possibility of retaliation; an opportunity to find closure. The one power you have as a victim over your abusers is your ability to offer them forgiveness in response to their offering of pain. Those that spend their energy causing misery in others' lives only do so because they want company. When love is extended in place of hatred, they realize they have no control over another's life. They realize their existence is a choice of their own. My words to Jubb were as follows:

I sit here in between two lives: the life of victimization and a life of survivorship.

These past three years, you've caused me to live the life of a victim. But that life is no more. This is the end of your reign of terror over my life and the lives of all those your hand had silenced.

You'll never truly know what it is to be innocently trapped. I wanted you to sit in a cage of someone's making and know what it feels to be truly trapped with no escape; a cage I sit in every night.

Alas, the justice system must take into account your "criminal career." As you have been a tax-paying, law abiding, upstanding citizen up to this point in life, no jail time can be expected.

But for me, it isn't that you haven't been convicted. It's that you've never been caught.

I used to hope you would adopt an apologetic heart, or truly any sign of remorse; I thought it would be easier for me to move forward.

I do believe the guilt that consumes you is so deeply depressed and denied, it has become penance enough.

This plight you now know, being generous, for another thirty years, is one that is self-constructed. I had no part in constructing your demise; I only acted as a shining light into your world of darkness – and I have at least another seventy years to heal from my burns and wounds.

But in order to heal, I can harbor no personal hatred or resentment toward someone who has been their source of suffering.

Your retribution has come. And now I can finally say I am finished. Your pain is in my past, as I truly hope the life you led before is for you.

Might I say, let us look with sanguine perspective toward what lies ahead – and I do hope, for all our lives, that is complete and comprehensive healing.

8

AFTERMATH

ureka! I always wanted to shout that.

Just like the kid on the playground that only wants to hear the words, "I'm sorry," all I ever wanted was a Eureka moment to scream "I told you so! I told you he was bad!" I only ever wanted one moment for those who had blamed me to have to admit, "you were right." I only ever wanted to hear someone take account-ability for casing me lifelong pain. The reality of moving past legal resolution is that there never really is, that moment. If your weight in moving past victimization is placed in being told you were in the right, that day will never come.

Regardless of the resolution found in a victim's legal case, it will take time for the reality that the lawsuit is over to manifest itself into the victim's outlook on life. They spent the last year, the last three years, in a constant state of wondering and unknowing, only to have the matter behind them in a matter of hours. It may feel as though the person they were before the victimization and before the legal roller coaster doesn't exist; they will need time to grieve the life that was lost the moment someone else exercised control over their life. All of this can be anticipated before resolution, but it is only once resolution has truly passed that these realities take root.

RELATIONSHIPS EVOLVE

It will take time for the victim to learn to talk about the lawsuit in terms of past. Tying in once again to setting expectations, this is why it is so important for a victim to establish the pillars of support needed to set themselves up for healing. These cornerstones are established, not only to support them through the legal process, but to help them transition into everyday life once the lawsuit has found resolution. When a person such as an attorney or a victims advocate or a member of the police department has been ever present through a victim's existence within the legal system, there can be new fear and dread that arises at the thought of these positions suddenly not existing. It's as if the end of their legal activity will suddenly end the care that was being shown to their circumstance. Ensuring that the victim is understanding of your job title and responsibilities toward their position as victim is vital to not only help them establish expectations for the system in the beginning, but it will help them understand the existence of your role and the need to minimize involvement once conclusion has been reached. When a victim can understand the nature of someone's job responsibilities and separate that from a personal relationship, one walking alongside the victim is able to negate any potential difficulty in establishing boundaries.

CRIMINAL LINGERING

As mentioned earlier, Jubb managed to never be found guilty of any account of sexual assault, only pleading no contest to two of the misdemeanor accounts; One of these even being dropped after he was found in good standing after eighteen months of probation. While I was aware that this charge would ultimately be dropped, at the time, I didn't understand the implications of what that meant. I didn't consider how I would feel once given the notification after he had been found in good standing after eighteen months and the charge was dropped. The morning that I was informed that the charge had indeed been dropped was the first-time post-trial that I felt my same mental feelings of victimization. I felt myself reliving the doubt that I had experienced all along the journey simply because it felt as if time was minimizing my experience. I didn't realize it would make me feel as though our justice system believes showing enough "good" can compensate for any amount of "bad." It is imperative a victim is walked through the real-life implications of legal aspects. Even if they are unable to grasp the impact such events will have on their life, receiving a baseline of what to expect when time comes will help them take ownership of their healing.

HUMAN BODY, SCORE KEEPER

Seeking understanding through the form of education sure of trauma can help a victim diminish feelings of doubt by understanding how their body operates. One of the books that was most influential in my understanding of my victim experience was *The Body Keeps the Score* by Bessel van Durkac. At the time I first picked up this book, I was struggling with a crippling state of compounded symptoms. I had isolated myself so that no one else could see the extent. In Chapter 17, van Durkac describes a conversation with a woman named Joan. Joan told the author "bulimia for her was what orgasms must be to other people and having sex with her husband for her was what vomiting must be like for others." Never before had I felt so validated.

When one finds themselves a victim of sexual assault, they find their state of fight or flight heightened in a permanent state thought of as hypervigilance. Because trauma intensifies memory and trauma impacts us on a biological level, our bodies are these incredible scorekeepers for what we have experienced. Our ability to learn from past situations and implement these lessons into future action is in our nature, just as animals learning about their environment. When one's body finds itself in the state of constant hypervigilance, it loses the ability to drive that state of dread down to its original baseline. Thinking back to our train example in the very beginning – hyper vigilance is the state of train cars racing chaotically over the tracks. The embody cannot determine when hypervigilance is necessary because it understands the state it was in before the unthinkable happened. If we know anything about Murphy's Law, we know that anything that can happen will. Thus, if you have evidence to prove that the unthinkable has happened to you at one point, it is only our system of logic to think that the unthinkable will happen again.

Understanding hypervigilance can best be done through understanding the three systems of our brain: reptilian, limbic, and neocortex. Our primitive self will always remain in the reptilian brain, concerned with ensuring that basic needs for life are met; ensuring that we have a safe place to sleep at night, that we have food when hungry, clean water when thirsty. Our emotional self-exist in the limbic system, accounting for the human we are through the storage of memory contributing to our personality to our behavior and emotional intelligence. These two systems act to guide and protect our main driver of a logic, our chief executive officer if you will, the neocortex. When the neocortex is influenced by a limbic system based on traumatic memory any emotional damage and a reptilian brain that is concerned with one's immediate safety, it creates a system of constant dread. Thus, a victim finds himself and a state unable to detach themselves from the feeling that something bad will happen in any given instant. Intentional effort must be taken to re-set these overactive command centers, intentional effort and sometimes, outside resources.

TOP-DOWN METHOD

The top-down approach refers to cognitively addressing the existence of the trauma. Be it through group therapy, individual session, or simple intention by the victim, there are many approaches toward bringing reason surrounding the changes trauma has had to one's individuality. Directly talking about the traumatic event itself or the aftermath that has on a victim's life will help develop a unified protocol within each of its brain systems surrounding the traumatic event. One of these approaches is known as the internal family systems approach, where a victim helps recognize the different managerial functions/actors/players within their psyche and the motivation for the existence of each player. Understanding that there is an internal security guard who is constantly patrolling the premises for any potential threat can help them pay attention to the existence of that function as an instinct. Understanding that there is a damaged childlike part of them that will always hide away and seek safety at all costs we'll help them interpret that behavior when it arises in daily habits. Despite how much attention one pays to attempting to understand the different operating systems that construct their psyche, one may be left with needing another approach Exclusively or supplementary.

Think of the top-down approach to processing trauma as logically outsmarting yourself; through reason and understanding, you are able to change the way you think and thus, change the way you respond to the world. While this is an important aspect of healing from sexual assault, one should not expect one method of healing to be an end-all-be-all. There is a time and place for everything.

MEDICATION

Medication is the second approach; chemically addressing the biological changes that a traumatic event has on the victim physically. When enduring a constant state of hypervigilance, the body cannot chemically find balance and thus, the systems are overridden chemically to help find balance. Some victims may choose to employee medication only in the instance of panic or on an as needed basis, occurring panic attacks or episodes of anxiety through benzodiazepines. Others may choose to rely upon SSRI's or selective serotonin reuptake in imitators, in order to find a constant level of stability surrounding their emotions. Both approaches to medication have the time and place that they are most effective. Victims should be reminded that it is their decision to determine what they need best for healing, given all the professional medical input has been made. Be aware. As with all things, we don't know until we know. Decisions to take medication or not, and even what medication is taken if determined to do so, may spur unforeseen emotion because of the cultural stigma surrounding mental health and the extended, those with PTSD.

BOTTOM UP

The bottom-up approach toward healing stems from addressing one's trauma through recreating positive physical-mental relationships. After trauma changes our biology recreating mental associations of the traumatic event offers new avenues for the body to create a physical connection to memory that will allow a victim to "tape over" negative past associations with positive new ones. There are countless ways to engage one's body with one's mind, think of the countless Olympic sports. Pick one and get busy. If intense activity isn't your scene, try pastime hobbies – one being theater. Engaging in avenues where the victim is allowed to embody the character of another can allow them to embody the powerful protector that was lacking during the incident of trauma. It will give them opportunity to embody whatever emotion they felt was lacking at the time – perhaps the confidence, or perhaps the vocal nature demanding attention from those in the room they wished they could have employed at the time that they felt voiceless. Theater, or actions of role play, don't have to exist on stage or through a hobby group; joining a community choir or even finding a secure person in which to role play sexual situations can offer a victim the scenario in which to change the outcome to that of a positive nature.

Regardless of the method, encourage your victimized clients to pay attention to their hypervigilance. Encourage them to identify their best practice for rewiring negative associations, to take ownership of their healing in pursuit of living as a survivor.

9

POTHOLES

rowing up in a place that paved roads, wait, what are paved roads? They didn't exist If they were once paved, they had been cracked and patched time and time over again so that it resembles more of Roman architecture than any project from the DOT. Most of the year, this wasn't an issue as the roads were paved snowy white with the snow that had started building up since the beginning of September. It wasn't until the breakup in May that the potholes painstakingly obvious. Even the most expert of drivers couldn't manage to circumvent every pothole that would be encountered and thus, there was always a frequent jolt in the cab.

As was evident from the moment I found myself standing beside Jubb in the lobby of the courthouse, even the most intentional advocate can overlook how certain aspects of the legal world impact the victim's experience. Unfortunately, it takes being a victim yourself of sexual violence to understand the degree to which victims experience impact in every area of their lives. Without ever experiencing sexual violence yourself, it is possible to be an empathetic advocate given intentional practice.

POST-TRAUMATIC STRESS INJURY

One of the biggest oversights amidst those interacting with victims of sexual assault is the mentality that PTSD is a mental illness and not as it should be renamed, PTSI, post-traumatic stress causes injury. This relationship with trauma causing physical injury is examined in *The Invisible Machine* by Dr. Eugene Lipov and Jamie Mustard. Dr. Lipov explains how hyper vigilance is a tool for our existence as humans, as most humans interact with smaller elements of trauma in an everyday sense but as the stress passes, our sympathetic nervous system returns to baseline. If our nervous system was dubbed and invisible machine, hypervigilance is the state of that machine always being on. He goes on to offer practical evidence that this system can be forced into reset through SGB therapy, or stellate ganglion block. One of the subjects of Dr. Lipov study and an active voice in the book is a man named Trevor. We shared an honest conversation over the phone in January 2023. A green beret who, perhaps experienced more trauma outside of military operation than while on duty, I was completely floored at the praise he employed surrounding the healing stemming from SGB treatment. He experienced sexual abuse from his stepfather for nearly ten years before his mother found out, as well as the existing factors of poverty and gang violence due to his socioeconomic status. After failed suicide attempts, he enlisted in the military before eventually being honored with the status of green beret and the honor of witness to violence that came along with such status. Trevor story through therapy with Dr. Lipov the truth surrounding the reality of post-traumatic stress causing physical injury instead of creating mental disorder.

DON'T TREAT ME LIKE A CHILD, JUST KIDDING, PLEASE DO

Another way in which those interacting with victims of sexual assault can fall into a pothole is by failing to understand a victim's ability to comprehend every aspect of this situation in which they find themselves. Every day we interact with elements of culture and society that we have no understanding of and thus, it is not too absurd to expect that victims engaging with the legal worlds are often engaging with such for the first time. Imagine the recipe for shoe pastry, a mindless chore to the owner of a patisserie but a daunting challenge to the occasional home Baker. Often those engaging with victims of sexual assaults failed to remember that they interact with victims on a daily sense but for the victim, this is an earth-shaking event that has changed the trajectory of their entire life. It becomes easy to assume an understanding of certain vocabulary or of institutional operation, or simply understanding that their life is not over and that things happiness life itself will still happen outside of the scope of their abuse. Yet, or the victim, the world is standing still. Approaching a victim with the empathy that this too shall pass can offer a victim security knowing that there is someone who has navigated this situation prior and successfully, but also with the validation that they have the right to take the title of victim while being encouraged to transform such a title into that of survivor.

While it is one side of the spectrum to approach a victim from a place where their understanding of the legal world is assumed, the other end is to engage with the victim as though they lack the ability to comprehend. Often those attempting to approach a victim from the place of empathy can do so in a manner that is demeaning to a victim's intelligence. There's a fine balance to be struck and identifying what areas the victim feels the most insecure so that education surrounding such areas can be offered without overwhelming with too much information or offering too little.

SO MUCH TO DO, SUCH LITTLE TIME

Even with the purest of intention, one can find developing an empathetic approach to their sexually assaulted clients is a daunting task. Perhaps it seems as though you don't have enough time to cater to the abundant needs of a specific client; perhaps they are seeking more under-standing than you can possibly facilitate. Maybe you've encountered a victim that challenges your confidence because of their uniquely complex situation. Whatever the case may be that is causing doubt you are capable of offering support, let that doubt lie. If all else fails, reach out to your own support pillars for direction, and if all else fails – you can always come to me.

10

EVER FORWARD

When you find yourself a gladiator in the life of the victim of sexual assault, it may feel as though there is no way for you to proceed without causing some amount of compounding damage toward their situation. It is vital that victims navigating legal structures be met with empathy in each professional position that offers a liaison between the language of that of the law and that of victim mentality. Educating oneself in the experience of a victim will enable advocates to guide victims through the legal system while avoiding a secondary assault.

EMBRACE THE SUCK

Setting expectations with the victim regarding your position in their journey to survivorship is crucial for helping a victim establish a firm foundation on which to build their healing. A victim is unable to fully engage with the legal system in which they are seeking justice until they have a baseline of expectations of what to expect from each system. Establishing expectations will also help them iden-tify avenues of support from an early point in the legal process, so that gaps in their support system can be filled before a victim has the opportunity to feel those needs are neglected. Establishing support around one physical, psychological, and personal fronts is essential to a victim's ability to build the foundation necessary for healing.

Once a victim makes a decision on how to proceed, it is crucial that they be offered education surrounding the institutions are in which they are engaging. There will be great impact to their daily life, and by establishing the right support system, they will be able to navigate new personal and health challenges. Given an understanding of the process, expectations for what is to come, and the proper support pillars established, a victim will be fully equipped to take ownership of their transformation from victim to survivor.

THE FOUR AGREEMENTS

The journey to develop one's survival skills is a life-long process. A victim will learn their own personal strategy for navigating the practical effects of their trauma. Mine derived from a multitude of readings and thought strategy put to the test.

Early in my high school basketball career, I found myself succumb to an injury stemming from torn ankle ligaments. Two years of physical therapy rendered little to no help, so I journeyed to the Mayo Clinic in Minnesota to have experts give their input. While in testing, the doctors found that I had a syndrome called wolf Parkinson's white (WPW). This heart defect present at birth stems from an extra electrical pathway between my left atrium and ventricle, causing an elevated heartbeat. The combination of receiving the WPW diagnosis and unable to change the circumstance of my leg injury, in addition to the reality that my aunt lives with debilitating MS And my mother with arthritis, made it painstakingly aware that I needed to focus on my physical health, regardless of the extent of my physical activity.

Community yoga teachers held sessions at the Recreation Center which offered me the opportunity to learn from a variety of practices. Many of the teachers leading sessions had come into their teaching practice through vast personal experience, and I often found myself lost in conversation after session had ended. Through one of these conversations came the suggestion for a book titled, *The Four Agreements*.

These four agreements have morphs with my worldview into four commitments I make with myself on a nearly daily basis.

BE INTENTIONAL WITH YOUR WORDS

Being intentional with one's words requires effort to slow the connection between one's mind and mouth; but this effort is well placed when we can ensure that the rhetoric we are employing accurately reflects the position we are trying to make. Humans fall victim to speaking too quickly or to letting emotions overwhelm the subject of thought. When we are intentional with our words, we create our accountability system so that when we articulate our thought, both subconscious self and external self, on the same page. In the era of tweets and statuses, talk can feel incredibly cheap. Anyone can publish their thoughts in an instant, and on the Internet, everything is forever. As victims, it can be incredibly easy to succumb to emotional speech. While it takes honest recognition of a victim's emotions in order to shed one's victim status, publicly making emotional comments can give ammunition to those criticizing any words said period. By committing to be intentional with one's words, a victim can engage with the public in confidence that what is being vocalized aligns with the reality of their needs.

DON'T TAKE THINGS PERSONALLY

As victims, it is incredibly easy to point to another's action and say, "You hurt me!" When you experience intentional harm from another, it becomes easy to assume the same in other's actions, even though malicious harm is rarely the case. Just driving down the road, we may ask ourselves, "Why did they cut me off?" As if the other person's action was intended to make us angry, when in reality, they were probably only thinking about themselves. Perhaps they did not see your vehicle because of sunlight or because of an obstruction, or perhaps they genuinely thought that they had time to make an entrance. When we make the assumption that other people's actions were intended to cause us pain and suffering, it becomes rather easy to walk through life considering yourself the center of the universe. Assuming that other people's actions were meant to cause us harm is frankly a selfish position. The world does not revolve around you, and it never will. This can be both a comforting and also daunting thought; but as victims, it is imperative that we learn to separate the things that happened to us from malicious intent.

DON'T MAKE ASSUMPTIONS

Aligned with the drive to not take things personally comes the intentional effort to not make assumptions. When we take things personally, we are assuming that the other person meant us harm. By committing to simply refrain from making assumptions in the first place, we enable ourselves to live free from actively reading into reality as though it were bad in nature. I may have taken this to an extreme extent in life as I seem to ask even the simplest questions because I never want to be found to assume. This can be as a simple effort as asking which direction the bathrooms are in to a server even if a glimpse of what may have been the restrooms was seen upon entrance. As to avoid walking aimlessly around amidst other tables and rushing wait staff. Perhaps your exercise of not making an assumption simply means asking your partner what they would like for dinner just confirming that previously determined plans were still in place. When we choose not to assume and to gain understanding, we are choosing to engage with those around us and encourage communication. By simply asking for verification instead of making an assumption, we are also indicating to the party being questioned that the issue is of importance, that even how minor we don't deem it trivial. When dealing with victims of sexual assault, providing the opportunity for them to articulate their perspective instead of those around them making assumptions for them enables them to gain control of their circumstance and develop the autonomy that may have felt overridden in the past.

ALWAYS DO YOUR BEST

When we have committed to being intentional with our words, committed to not taking life personally and committed toward not making assumptions of other's actions or simple factors of reality, we are then able to commit ourselves to giving of our best at any given point.

Upon first thought of always doing your best one may feel that this is an unachievable agreement to make with oneself. Committing to always doing your best means that given the factors of time and place, you give up yourself in a manner that when looking back, there will be no grounds for you to say I could have done more. Some days committing to doing your best will look as that of simply showing up, of being a warm body, and getting through the day in one complete piece. There are many days in which I have found it an incredible achievement to simply survive twenty-four hours longer. When I look back on those days, I looked to my victim myself with immense compassion knowing that that was the best I could give at the time. Being able to find appreciation for the times in which we have only the means to meet our basic needs allows us to find renewed motivation for the times and which our energy is at max capacity.

BAREFOOT MOUNTAIN CLIMBING

"You have any plans Wednesday night? I was thinking of climbing Pyramid Mountain. in dresses." This is a text I received from my doctor while living back in my hometown of Kodiak for a brief time in 2021. I first met Shana while I was living in Nome, attending high school. She was my primary care doctor when I was sixteen and who helped me with all the first female appointments a girl goes through before moving to Oregon in 2016. Since our first office visit, I struck a chord with Shana because of her vibrant outlook on life and her ability to install female confidence from our divine nature as woman. Fast forward to a chilly February day in 2021 when I was sitting in a truck waiting for my COVID shot, a doctor in full PPE walks by with an oddly familiar pair of braids and that certain style of headband – I asked the long-respected Dr. Kohler if by chance the other that doctor walking by his name was Shauna. While all I could see was his eyes, his reaction was stunned as he nodded yes. I knew it could be no other, and as soon as she turned around, I waved in her direction and she flew over giving me the biggest hug I had had since the onset of COVID a year prior. From that moment forward, Shawna became monumental in helping me navigate a difficult time surrounding my existence as a victim.

This text I received about my plans for Wednesday night was not out of the ordinary; but when we got to the base of the mountain, we did decide to do something rather outside the box. We indeed were wearing dresses as per her request. She had told me in the text that I was always wearing dresses and she admired how I never let then stop me from being physically active and if I could do so on an everyday basis we could do so climbing and mountain. This was all on par, it was her suggestion to climb the mountain barefoot that threw me for a loop. Para mountain was named as such because of the triangular shape to the top half of the mountain. The nature of this mountain was also the reason that my mother had named her small home school cohort pyramid mountain Academy. I had long been given the image as a kid of life being like a mountain climb, full of treacherous terrain, unforeseen challenge, harsh weather, but gorgeous views. And here my doctor was suggesting that we do it all with bare feet! Ultimately, she made the trek both ways barefoot while I opted to trek up the mountain with my Keen's firmly laced but descended the mountain as such of a goat, bare foot. Truth be told I would make the choice again because descending the mountain what have resulted in my twisted ankle as we stayed at the summit to watch sunset. There were countless sections where I had to made strategic lateral movements in order to achieve the ultimate horizontal objective.

This is true in our legal pursuits.

This is true in our pursuit through life.

Sometimes, we must sacrifice obvious progress for a more strategic position.

Shana's influence in my life was much greater than simply asking me to join her on mountain summits. Shana was the one who gave me the book, *Loving What Is by* Byron Katie. Here, the reader is lead through the practice of deciphering the true nature of one's fears by asking four simple questions. Overtime, her worksheets and questions have morphed themselves with my development of understanding how to process once trauma by paying attention to what exists. There's a beautiful skill in the nature of recognizing reality and not demeaning it as good or bad, as it lending positive or negative energy, but it's simply being. As humans we have a finite amount of energy that we can put toward achieving our goals and accomplishing daily tasks to perpetuate life; when we put the resource of energy toward circumstance that we have no control over or human choice that we have no influence on, we are wasting our resources. Every morning one should commit to putting forth energy into the situations in which they have the ability to influence and learn to accept that which they do not. Is it not the serenity prayer that states quotation God grant me the serenity to accept the things I cannot change courage to change the things I can and wisdom to know the difference."

These are the questions I ask myself to find the clarity and power to move forward when faced with difficult thought: Do I have evidence that this is true?

Do I have the power to affect the outcome?

When we realize we are powerless in our circumstance, there is but one power move we have yet to play.

Embrace the suck.

When we choose to embrace our circumstances, we are choosing to take ownership over our reaction to the world. Circumstance is a perspective, choose to alter your perspective through intentional effort.

I think back to the room where I sat amidst the three attorneys. Had it not been for the empathy offered by the second two, I would not have developed the skill to take ownership over my reactions to the world. Had it not been for empathy shown by my attorneys, I would not have developed my skill to walk away from the life of a victim and claim my identify as survivor.

YOU FOUND GOLD

I can't thank you enough for giving me your attention though the last pages. Your commitment to implementing trauma informed practices is the key to ensuring empathetic advocacy thought the legal process. Much like the gold-riddled earth around my home in Nome, Alaska, I've hidden a webpage on my site. Here, you who have taken advancements to become more empathetic are celebrated and offered opportunity to connect with others who have taken the same steps. Thank you for the gold that is YOU!

www.AnnaMarieMotis.com/helpers

ACKNOWLEDGMENTS

To Jacob – You reinstalled my confidence in chivalry while upsetting my views of norms. You gave me more love and patience than I probably deserved. Thank you for reminding me of all the truths I had forgotten. Thank you for convincing me of selfless love. Thank you for enduring with me till the end.

To Cory – No words could be used, no words need be used! Thank you for understanding my questions before they even become thoughts; thank you for anchoring me these last few months.

To Julie – Your existence in my world has brought more equilibrium than you'll ever know. Thank you for sincerely listening; for offering insight from your perspective with my own reasoning. Thank you for teaching me the difference between the time to embrace tears and the time to tell yourself to cry tomorrow.

To Ashton – Your expertise in all things technical has provided tremendous assurance in a world I feel so foreign. Thank you for embracing all my unique specificity. Thank you for offering encouragement to step beyond what I think is possible.

To the Difference Press Family, Angela – My salvation after so long! Thank you for offering tangible steps forward, invaluable expertise when in need and encouragement at every step.

To the Linfield Community – Each of you have played a monumental role in shaping the construction of my worldview. I'm grateful for the experience offered from every interaction, every class taken, every position held, every person encountered. Thank you, faculty, for teaching me to consider the real life implications of that which is theorized. Thank you, students, for teaching me learning happens outside the classroom just as much as within. Thank you, staff, for teaching me the importance of leading by example. Thank you, administration, for teaching me the importance of standing resilient with integrity.

To my Health Care Team – Your compassionate attention to my physical needs has healed more than is reflected in your charts. Thank you for giving me renewed and sustainable strength and confidence. Thank you, Dr. Waldorf, for bringing back my smile and vibrancy. Thank you, Patty, for reminding me life is a Cuisinart; for being my lighthouse when I could hardly keep afloat. Thank you, Doug, for offering relief and validation when I had surrendered to my status quo. So many more of you have been integral to my healing. Thank you, everyone.

To my Kodiak Family, Doreece, and Sam – You have held my hand since ever I could remember. You have shown me generosity beyond that which I'm even aware. Thank you for taking me under your wing; thank you for loving me as one of your own.

To my Homer Family, Elissa and Beth – The time we shared riding bareback up the hill were some of the happiest moments of my adolescence. Thank you for bringing me back to those moments when it feels like they've been lost forever. Thank you for your sisterhood through all phases of life.

To my Nome Family, Senora and Kailey – We share experiences unbelievable to most. Thank you for teaching me the value of community, of honoring those that contribute to our development.

To the Hitchcock Family – You'll never know the impact of your kindness. Thank you for being my rescue.

To my Basketball Family, Casey – You recognized my desire to extend care and gave me the opportunity to feel a member of the team. Thank you for teaching me mental toughness before I understood the value of such a term. Thank you for teaching me the importance of reminding people they are appreciated.

To the Kiff Family – You adopted me as if my last initial was K since your son called me friend; I can't begin to express the depth of my love for each of you. Thank you for taking me as I am and caring beyond definitions.

To my Parents, Tim and Stacie – Just to know you're proud I'm your daughter is all I'll ever ask. Thank you for raising me to be Christlike; it's because of the empathy for others you installed that I have the capacity to love as I do.

To Charlie – You bring immense joy to all in the house. Thank you for keeping Dad and Mom young and on their toes.

To Jenae – You are inspiration to us all that we set our own limitations. Thank you for showing us how powerful we can be when we forget about expectations.

To Jenessa – You remind us all to stop and enjoy the simple beauties of life. Thank you for filling the house with music.

To Aaron – I will always want to care and protect you as my baby brother. Thank you for reminding me not to take life too seriously. Thank you for sharing my love of Red Bull. Thank you for always giving the most thoughtful gifts.

To Jonathan – When I have been most lost, most afraid, most alone, your voice could always be heard. The best gift in life I could have received was that of my older brother. Thank you for always picking up the phone. Thank you for showing me mental toughness. Thank you for not letting me forget I am capable of rising above.

To Michelle – You are the strongest woman I know. Thank you for grounding Jonathan, and through him, for grounding myself.

To Eleanor – My sweet Marie; you will always be my little ducky. I cannot wait to take you along on my travels. Thank you giving us the gift of seeing your mom and dad as parents for the first time. Thank you for first showing me the joys of being Auntie.

To Molly – My dearest little mirror; I can only imagine the tough conversations we will have in the future. The world is a difficult place for those of us with such specific ideals. Thank you for reminding me to stay stubborn. I cannot wait to lend you my listening ear.

To Hannah – My perfect little bug; you tie us all together. Thank you for already bringing such laughter and unity into our lives. I cannot wait to indulge your curiosities.

To Jason – Oh, how I value how you embrace and encourage examination of the contrary. Thank you for calling, every single time.

To Nic – You extended me validation and invigoration through the bitter end. Thank you for being a kindred spirit.

To Claudia – Your optimism is a constant source of inspiration. Thank you for being such a strong force of positivity. Thank you for bringing Ellie in our lives.

To Morgan – Your talent never ceases to astound me. Thank you for always offering creative solutions. Thank you for always framing me in my best light.

To Kainoa – There are few who understand my

Linfield experience more intimately than you. Thank you for sharing all the experiences, the chaos and learning curves of young leadership. Thank you for reminding me my mind is just a little different and that's OK.

To Israel – You have inspired so much critical thought; my external brain. Thank you for the space our friendship provides, for the global adventures it leads us through. Thank you for teaching me to embrace the experience (even the floor of a railcar).

To Beth and Chris – Educational and Recreational; you are the best of both parts of my life! Thank you for accepting me with all my, corks, quirks? Thank you for reminding me to laugh in the face of tragedy, teaching me to tenaciously cling to what I know to be true.

To Robin – You gave me love when I was most broken without ever indicating I was the one to blame. Thank you for teaching me the importance of habits. Thank you for teaching me the importance of honesty with self. Thank you for teaching me how to use salt properly.

To James and Brandy – You are the reason this book is a reality. It was you who brought comprehensive healing. Thank you for giving me traction. Thank you for helping me understand unconditional love in abundance.

To Sean – You offered me structure when my world was collapsing. For 987 straight days, you remained my anchor in the raging storm. Thank you for giving hope to those in the deepest of despairs. Thank you for bringing the reckoning.

To Erin – You are the voice I always need to hear. You taught me the importance of paying attention to our pain, if only to understand how to better advocate. Thank you for being my mirror. Thank you for living the example of the empathetic attorney.

GLOSSARY

This glossary is intended to offer insight as to what legal basic terminology a victim may encounter to provide a baseline of understanding. Definitions have been written incorporating the necessary legal information while keeping the scope focused on information pertinent to the victim's experience.

1. Acquittal – Judgment that a criminal defendant has not been proven guilty beyond a reasonable doubt.
2. Affidavit – A written statement of facts confirmed by the oath of the party making it. Affidavits must be notarized or administered by an officer of the court with such authority.
3. Allegation – Something that someone says happened.
4. Appeal – A request made after a trial, asking another court (usually the court of appeals) to decide whether the trial was conducted properly. To make such a request is "to appeal" or "to take an appeal." Both the plaintiff and the defendant can appeal, and the party doing so is called the appellant. Appeals can be made for a variety of reasons including improper procedure and asking the court to change its interpretation of the law.

5. Arraignment – A proceeding in which an individual who is accused of committing a crime is brought into court, told of the charges, and asked to plead guilty or not guilty.
6. Arrest Warrant – A written order directing the arrest of a party. Arrest warrants are issued by a judge after a showing of probable cause.
7. Assault – an intentional act that puts another person in reasonable apprehension of imminent harmful or offensive contact.
8. Battery – an intentional tort committed when a person intentionally causes harm or offensive contact with another person.
9. Bail – Security given for the release of a criminal defendant or witness from legal custody (usually in the form of money) to secure his/her appearance on the day and time appointed.
10. Bench Trial – Trial without a jury in which a judge decides the facts. In a jury trial, the jury decides the facts. Defendants will occasionally waive the right to a jury trial and choose to have a bench trial.
11. Burden of Proof – describes the standard to which the appropriate party must prove their claim. In Civil cases, this is met upon a preponderance of the evidence, meaning the plaintiff merely needs to prove the alleged action was more likely to have happened than to have not. In criminal cases, this standard is raised to prove the defendant's guilt beyond reasonable doubt.
12. Case Law – The use of court decisions to determine how other law (such as statutes) should apply in a given situation. For example, a

trial court may use a prior decision from the Supreme Court that has similar issues.

13. Charge – The specific law that the police believe the defendant has broken.

14. Circumstantial Evidence – All evidence that is not direct evidence (such as eyewitness testimony).

15. Coercion – (A) threats of serious harm to or physical restraint against any person; (B) any scheme, plan, or pattern intended to cause a person to believe that failure to perform an act would result in serious harm to or physical restraint against any person; or (C) the abuse or threatened abuse of law or the legal process.

16. Common Law – The legal system that originated in England and is now in use in the United States. It is based on court decisions rather than statutes passed by the legislature.

17. Complaint – A written statement by the plaintiff stating the wrongs allegedly committed by the defendant.

18. Consent – a person voluntarily and willfully agrees to another's proposition. Consent cannot be legally given when an individual is known to be under the influence or in a mentally impaired state.

19. Conviction – A judgment of guilt against a criminal defendant.

20. Counsel – Legal advice; a term used to refer to lawyers in a case.

21. Counterclaim – A claim that a defendant makes against a plaintiff. Counterclaims can often be brought within the same proceedings as the plaintiff's claims.

22. Criminal Defendant – a person who has been charged with committing a crime.
23. Criminal Procedure – the federal or state system of applying established law through governing proceedings to determine responsibility and apply punishment of wrongdoings.
24. Civil Procedure – the federal or state system of settling dispute among disagreeing parties.
25. Cross-examine – Questioning of a witness by the attorney for the other side.
26. Damages – Money paid by defendants to successful plaintiffs in civil cases to compensate the plaintiffs for their injuries.
27. Defendant – In a civil suit, the person complained against; in a criminal case, the person accused of the crime.
28. Defense – the rationale employed to protect the defendant's position
29. Deposition – An oral statement made before an officer authorized by law to administer oaths. Such statements are often taken to examine potential witnesses, to obtain discovery, or to be used later in trial.
30. Direct Evidence – Evidence that supports a fact without an inference.
31. Discovery – Lawyers' examination, before trial, of facts and documents in possession of the opponents to help the lawyers prepare for trial.
32. Docket – A log containing brief entries of court proceedings.
33. Evidence – Information presented in testimony or in documents that is used to persuade the fact finder (judge or jury) to decide the case for one side or the other.

34. Exculpatory Evidence – Evidence which tends to show the defendant's innocence.
35. Exhibit – Physical evidence or documents that are presented in a court proceeding. Common exhibits include contracts, weapons, and photographs.
36. Federal – relating to the national system of governance, applying to all states and territories.
37. Felony – A crime carrying a penalty of more than a year in prison.
38. File – To place a paper in the official custody of the clerk of court to enter into the files or records of a case. Lawyers must file a variety of documents throughout the life of a case.
39. Force – the use of a weapon, the use of physical strength or violence as sufficient to overcome, restrain, or injure a person, or inflicting physical harm sufficient to coerce or compel submission by the victim.
40. Grand Jury – A body of citizens who listen to evidence of criminal allegations, which are presented by the government, and determines whether there is probable cause to believe the offense was committed. As it is used in federal criminal cases, "the government" refers to the lawyers of the U.S. Attorney's office who are prosecuting the case. Grand jury proceedings are closed to the public, and the person suspected of having committed the crime is not entitled to be present or have an attorney present. States are not required to use grand juries, but the federal government must do so under the Constitution.
41. Grievous Bodily Harm – serious bodily injury. It includes fractured or dislocated bones, deep

cuts, torn members of the body, serious damage to internal organs, and other severe bodily injuries. It does not include minor injuries such as a black eye or a bloody nose.

42. Guilty – Admission by a defendant that they have committed the crime they were charged with, or the finding by a judge or a jury that the defendant has committed the crime.

43. Habeas Corpus – A writ that is often used to bring a prisoner before the court to determine the legality of his imprisonment. A prisoner wanting to argue that there is not sufficient cause to be imprisoned would file a writ of habeas corpus. It may also be used to bring a person in custody before the court to give testimony, or to be prosecuted.

44. Hearsay – Statements by a witness who did not see or hear the incident in question but learned about it through secondhand information such as another's statement, a newspaper, or a document. Hearsay is usually not admissible as evidence in court, but there are many exceptions to that rule.

45. Impeachment – The process of calling something into question, as in "impeaching the testimony of a witness."

46. Inculpatory Evidence – Evidence which tends to show the defendant's guilt.

47. Incest – sexual contact between blood relatives, regardless of consent.

48. Indictment – The formal charge issued by a grand jury stating that there is enough evidence that the defendant committed the crime to

justify having a trial; it is used primarily for felonies. Can also refer to the Initial Hearing.

49. Initial Hearing – Court proceeding in which the defendant learns of his rights and the charges against him and the judge decides bail. Can also refer to the Indictment.

50. Injunction – An order of the court prohibiting (or compelling) the performance of a specific act to prevent irreparable damage or injury.

51. Interview – A meeting with the police, prosecutor or investigator.

52. Judge – Government official with authority to decide lawsuits brought before courts. Judicial officers of the highest court in each state are called justices.

53. Judgement – The official decision of a court finally determining the respective rights and claims of the parties to a suit.

54. Jurisdiction – (1) The legal authority of a court to hear and decide a case. Concurrent jurisdiction exists when two courts have simultaneous responsibility for the same case. Some issues can be heard in both state and federal courts. The plaintiff initially decides where to bring the suit, but in some cases, the defendant can seek to change the court. (2) The geographic area over which the court has authority to decide cases. A federal court in one state, for example, can usually only decide a case that arose from actions in that state.

55. Juror – A person who is on the jury.

56. Jury – Persons selected according to law and sworn to inquire into and declare a verdict on matters of fact. State court juries can be as small

as six jurors in some cases. Federal juries for civil suits must have six jurors, and criminal suits must have twelve.

57. Jury Pool – The group of people from which the actual jury is chosen. The jury pool is randomly selected from a source such as voter registration banks. Lawyers in the case choose the actual jurors from the jury pool through a process called voir dire.

58. Lawsuit – A legal action started by a plaintiff against a defendant based on a complaint that the defendant failed to perform a legal duty, resulting in harm to the plaintiff.

59. Litigation – A case, controversy, or lawsuit. Participants (plaintiffs and defendants) in lawsuits are called litigants.

60. Misdemeanor – Usually a petty offense, a less serious crime than a felony, punishable by less than a year of confinement.

61. Mistrial – An invalid trial caused by fundamental error. When a mistrial is declared, the trial must start again, beginning with the selection of a new jury.

62. Motion – Attempt to have a limited issue heard by the court. Motions can be filed before, during, and after trial.

63. Nolo Contendere – No contest. Has the same effect as a plea of guilty as far as the criminal sentence is concerned, but the plea may not be considered an admission of guilt for any other purpose. Sometimes, a guilty plea could later be used to show fault in a lawsuit, but the plea of nolo contendere forces the plaintiff in the

lawsuit to prove that the defendant committed the crime.

64. Oath – A promise to tell the truth.
65. Objection – A protest by an attorney, challenging a statement or question made at trial. Common objections include an attorney "leading the witness" or a witness making a statement that is hearsay. Once an objection is made, the judge must decide whether to allow the question or statement.
66. Opinion – A judge's written explanation of a decision of the court. In an appeal, multiple opinions may be written. The court's ruling comes from a majority of judges and forms the majority opinion. A dissenting opinion disagrees with the majority because of the reasoning and/or the principles of law on which the decision is based. A concurring opinion agrees with the result of the court but offers further comment possibly because they disagree with how the court reached its conclusion.
67. Oral Argument – An opportunity for lawyers to summarize their position before the court in an appeal and also to answer the judges' questions.
68. Parties – Plaintiffs and defendants (petitioners and respondents) to lawsuits, also known as appellants and appellees in appeals, and their lawyers.
69. Perpetrator – a person who committed a crime.
70. Petit Jury – A group of citizens who hear the evidence presented by both sides at trial and determine the facts in dispute. Federal criminal juries consist of twelve persons. Federal civil

juries consist of six persons. Also known as Trial Jury.

71. Plaintiff – The person who files the complaint in a civil lawsuit.

72. Plea – In a criminal case, the defendant's statement pleading "guilty" or "not guilty" in answer to the charges in open court. A plea of nolo contendere or an Alford plea may also be made. A guilty plea allows the defendant to forego a trial.

73. Plea Deal – Agreement between the defendant and prosecutor where the defendant pleads guilty in exchange for a concession by the prosecutor. It may include lesser charges, a dismissal of charges, or the prosecutor's recommendation to the judge of a more lenient sentence. Also known as a Plea Bargain or Plea Agreement.

74. Pleadings – Written statements of the parties in a civil case of their positions. In federal courts, the principal pleadings are the complaint and the answer.

75. Precedent – A court decision in an earlier case with facts and law similar to a dispute currently before a court. Precedent will ordinarily govern the decision of a later similar case, unless a party can show that it was wrongly decided or that it differed in some significant way. Some precedent is binding, meaning that it must be followed. Other precedents need not be followed by the court but can be considered influential.

76. Procedure – The rules for the conduct of a lawsuit; there are rules of civil, criminal, evidence, bankruptcy, and appellate procedure.

77. Preliminary Hearing – A hearing where the judge decides whether there is enough evidence to require the defendant to go to trial. Preliminary hearings do not require the same rules as trials. For example, hearsay is often admissible during the preliminary hearing but not at trial.

78. Pretrial Conference – A meeting of the judge and lawyers to discuss which matters should be presented to the jury, to review evidence and witnesses, to set a timetable, and to discuss the settlement of the case.

79. Probable Cause – An amount of suspicion leading one to believe certain facts are probably true. The Fourth Amendment requires probable cause for the issuance of an arrest or search warrant.

80. Probation – A sentencing alternative to imprisonment in which the court releases convicted defendants under supervision as long as certain conditions are observed.

81. Prosecute – To charge someone with a crime. A prosecutor tries a criminal case on behalf of the government.

82. Public Defender – Represent defendants who can't afford an attorney in criminal matters.

83. Rape – the penetration, no matter how slight, of the vagina or anus, with any body part or physical object or by oral penetration by a sex organ of another person, done so without consent.

84. Record – A written account of all the acts and proceedings in a lawsuit.

85. Restraining Order – a legally binding court order issued to protect a victim from any type of abuse, threat or harassment.

86. Sentence – The punishment ordered by a court for a defendant convicted of a crime. Federal courts look to the United States Sentencing Commission Guidelines when deciding the proper punishment for a given crime.

87. Settlement – Parties to a lawsuit resolve their difference without having a trial. Settlements often involve the payment of compensation by one party in satisfaction of the other party's claims.

88. Sexual Assault – the contact or penetration, however slight, of the vulva or penis or anus of another by any part of the body or any object, with an intent to abuse, humiliate, harass, or degrade any person or to arouse or gratify the sexual desire of any person.

89. Sexual Contact – touching, or causing another person to touch, either directly or through the clothing, the vulva, penis, scrotum, anus, groin, breast, inner thigh, or buttocks of any person, with an intent to abuse, humiliate, harass, or degrade any person or to arouse or gratify the sexual desire of any person.

90. Sidebar – A conference between the judge and lawyers held out of earshot of the jury and spectators.

91. Statement – A description that a witness gives to the police and that the police write down.

92. Statute – A law passed by a legislature.

93. Statute of Limitations – A law that sets the time

within which parties must take action to enforce their rights.

94. Stay – A temporary pause or suspension of a judicial proceeding. Stays are usually designed to terminate upon the completion of specified event (e.g., a judicial decision in a separate case or the end of a government shutdown) or after a specific period of time.

95. Subpoena – A command to a witness to appear and give testimony.

96. Summary Judgement – A decision made on the basis of statements and evidence presented for the record without a trial. It is used when there is no dispute as to the facts of the case, and one party is entitled to judgment as a matter of law.

97. Testify – Answer questions in court.

98. Testimony – Evidence presented orally by witnesses during trials or before grand juries.

99. Tort – A civil wrong or breach of a duty to another person as outlined by law. A common tort is negligent operation of a motor vehicle that results in property damage and personal injury in an automobile accident.

100. Trial – A hearing that takes place when the defendant pleads "not guilty," and the parties are required to come to court to present evidence.

101. Verdict – The decision of a petit jury or a judge.

102. Voir Dire – The process by which judges and lawyers select a petit jury from among those eligible to serve by questioning them to determine knowledge of the facts of the case and a willingness to decide the case only on the evidence presented in court. "Voir dire" is a phrase meaning "to speak the truth."

103. Warrant – An arrest warrant is a written order directing the arrest of a party. A search warrant orders that a specific location be searched for items, which if found, can be used in court as evidence. Search warrants require probable cause in order to be issued.

104. Witness – A person called upon by either side in a lawsuit to give testimony before the court or jury.

ABOUT THE AUTHOR

An advocate, writer, and lobbyist, AnnaMarie Motis is the founder of Sangreene Solutions. Transforming her unbelievable upbringing on the edge of the arctic, finding herself a fully-voting university trustee by the age of twenty-one, and navigating multiple, multipronged legal pursuits by the age of twenty-five, AnnaMarie lends invaluable perspective through the eyes of a youngster with immense life experience.

Since finding herself victim of sexual violence at age thirteen, AnnaMarie has held a tenacious passion for bringing voice to the voiceless; but it wasn't until finding herself at the center of the Linfield College Scandal in 2019 that she ultimately focused her energy towards promoting a greater understanding of trauma.

AnnaMarie has worked with non-profit and religious organizations aimed at providing relief for individuals experiencing all forms of sexual violence. During her undergraduate career, she held more than sixteen separate paid or leadership positions across campus. These positions have exposed her to the conflicting needs between student interest and administrative necessity, victim experience and constitutional obligation. Her continued commitment to understanding of trauma has given her unique talent in navigating high-tension scenarios, from exam room to boardroom to courtroom.

Born on Kodiak Island, AnnaMarie has lived in Kenai, Soldotna, Homer, and Fairbanks aside from the five years spent in Nome, Alaska. She often attributes her relentless ingenuity in all aspects of life to lessons taught through life in The Great Land. Don't let her velvet dresses fool you - those XtraTuf's will carry her through any crisis life – or her clients – bring her way.

When not writing, she can be found making wine as "The Assistant to the Winemaker" at Chris James Cellars. When not wine-ing, she's probably whining to her twin black cats, Caster and Pollux. If not writing, wining or whining, she's racking her brain for another verb that starts with W.

ABOUT DIFFERENCE PRESS

Difference Press is the publishing arm of The Author Incubator, an Inc. 500 award-winning company that helps business owners and executives grow their brand, establish thought leadership, and get customers, clients, and highly-paid speaking opportunities, through writing and publishing books.

While traditional publishers require that you already have a large following to guarantee they make money from sales to your existing list, our approach is focused on using a book to grow your following – even if you currently don't have a following. This is why we charge an up-front fee but never take a percentage of revenue you earn from your book.

☞ MORE THAN A COACH. MORE THAN A PUBLISHER. ✍

We work intimately and personally with each of our authors to develop a revenue-generating strategy for the book. By using a Lean Startup style methodology, we guarantee the book's success before we even start writing. We provide all the technical support authors need with editing, design, marketing, and publishing, the emotional support you would get from a book coach to help you manage anxiety and time constraints, and we serve as a strategic thought partner engineering the book for success.

The Author Incubator has helped almost 2,000 entrepreneurs write, publish, and promote their non-fiction books. Our authors have used their books to gain international media exposure, build a brand and marketing following, get lucrative speaking engagements, raise awareness of their product or service, and attract clients and customers.

☞ ARE YOU READY TO WRITE A BOOK? ✍

As a client, we will work with you to make sure your book gets done right and that it gets done quickly. The Author Incubator provides one-stop for strategic book consultation, author coaching to manage writer's block and anxiety, full-service professional editing, design, and self-publishing services, and book marketing and launch campaigns. We sell this as one package so our clients are not slowed down with contradictory advice. We have a 99 percent success rate with nearly all of our clients completing their books, publishing them, and reaching bestseller status upon launch.

☞ APPLY NOW AND BE OUR NEXT SUCCESS STORY ✍

To find out if there is a significant ROI for you to write a book, get on our calendar by completing an application at www.TheAuthorIncubator.com/apply.

OTHER BOOKS BY DIFFERENCE PRESS

Fundraising without Burnout: Radically Reimagining Philanthropy to Transform Your Impact by Radha Friedman

22 Millionaire Money Codes: Create a 7-Figure Legacy Business as a Real Estate Professional by Connie Grant

Always Bring Your Sunglasses: And Other Stories from a Life of Sensory and Social Invalidation by Becca Lory Hector

Art of the Heart: The Doctor-Patient Partnership by Jay H. Kleiman, MD

Living Intentionally after Loss: 8 Steps to Reclaiming Your Passion and Purpose by Maya Manseau

Breakthrough to Entrepreneurial Brilliance: Shatter the Invisible Barrier Holding Your Business Back by Alana Mills

Is This a Cult?: Confronting the Line between Transformation and Exploitation by Anne. L. Peterson

Founder to Exit: A CFO's Blueprint for Small Business Owners by Pam Prior

Prove Them Wrong: One Immigrant's 10-Year Journey from Bankrupt to Millionaire by Héctor E. Quiroga, J.D.

A Second Wind after Loss: A Guide to Health and Renewed Purpose for the Grieving Heart by Denise Sherman

THANK YOU!

I can't thank you enough for giving me your attention though the last pages. Your commitment to implementing trauma informed practices is the key to ensuring empathetic advocacy thought the legal process. Much like the gold-riddled earth around my home in Nome, Alaska, I've hidden a webpage on my site. Here, you who have taken advancements to become more empathetic are celebrated and offered opportunity to connect with others who have taken the same steps. Thank you for the gold that is YOU!

www.AnnaMarieMotis.com/helpers